THE BIBLE DECODED

breaking the ancient code

Sandra L Butler

Copyright © 1999

All rights reserved including the right of reproduction
in whole or part in any form.

Library of Congress cataloging in Publication data:

Butler, Sandra L.
The Bible Decoded
ISBN-9780967729688

2020 Final Edition
ISBN-9780578815473

Published by
Gilead Publishing Company

Cover Design by Creative Image Design, Bozeman, Montana

This book is dedicated to
GILBERT L. STILES

Truth is what stands the test of experience.
Albert Einstein

Table of Contents

Foreword..vi

Introduction..vii

Chapter One — The Godhead..................................1

Chapter Two — Israel...19

Chapter Three — Judah..31

Chapter Four — Israel of the Gentiles...................57

Chapter Five — Judah of the Gentiles...................75

Chapter Six — Zion..93

Chapter Seven — Babylon....................................115

Chapter Eight — Jerusalem..................................135

Chapter Nine — The Great Tribulation...............145

Chapter Ten — The Passover................................155

Chapter Eleven — The Two Kingdoms................169

Chapter Twelve — The Two Resurrections.........187

Chapter Thirteen — The Joseph Story................199

Book References...225

Index to Scripture References..............................226

Foreword

There is a communication that is able to take place with God when one has no preconceived ideas about God. I first learned of such a communication back in 1975 when I met up with a man, living in his woodworking shop, sleeping on a cot in a space no bigger than a closet. He impressed upon me a most wonderful revelation, which he began receiving back in 1960. Having very little knowledge of the Bible, his mind served as a pure conduit. Over a period of fourteen years, he received a foundation of teachings baring little resemblance to those of mainstream religion. So intrigued by these teachings, I spent the next nineteen years with this man, taking lots of notes, filling one notebook after another until his death in the fall of 1994. And although he taught a knowledge that was unknown to the churches, he made it clear to his students that there was an even deeper level, and that it was up to them to tread it out. In the spring of 1997, I began a quest for this deeper truth, experiencing a series of events that prepared me for a direct communication with God, taking place over a period of seven years, between 1998 and 2005. What I received was a revelation of the symbolic code of the Bible.

Introduction

THE BIBLE DECODED provides us with an in-depth understanding of the symbolic code of the Bible. You will take a journey with the chosen people, the children of Israel, chosen out of all nations to teach us about ourselves, their journey a pattern of our life journey. Through revelation and word meaning you will learn God's spiritual language, the ancient code of the Bible, revealing the psychology of scripture through its symbolism. The stories of the Bible offer opportunities for growth. As we grow in our knowledge of the ancient spiritual Word of God through a decoding of the scriptures, we are given an opportunity to grow in spiritual essence through the application of the works contained therein. The Patriarchs lay out God's ancient instruction, which if followed will bring us back to that elevated state of existence once known to Adam and Eve, and that we once knew as little children. The Prophets serve to reveal the error that caused us to fall from this perfected spiritual state, while warning us of the physical and spiritual consequences of that error. The names of the people, places, and things contained in the Bible, many of which share the same symbolic meaning, reveal God's end of day's message to His children. And we, being spiritual children, unskilled and disobedient with respect to the spiritual word and works of God, must be told again and again, which has been brilliantly accomplished through the intriguing, and sometimes perplexing stories of the Bible.

Chapter One
The Godhead

In the beginning God created the heaven and the earth. God created heaven and earth in His mind through the faculty of thought. The same way a building is designed before it is built, God being the architect. *And the earth was without form, and void; and darkness was upon the face of the deep.* The earth was without form as it had not yet been made. Before anything is made, there is an idea, a thought. This is the beginning of creation. Then energy is applied to that thought. *And the Spirit of God moved.* The Energy of God moved upon His thought. The energy we put into a thought is the first stage in bringing what we think into our reality, bringing it into existence. *And God said, Let there be light: and there was light.* God spoke, the word being the builder. The word is the works that are applied in order for the idea or concept created in the mind to begin its formation; the process by which something evolves. The first thought to evolve or be formed and brought into existence was light, the means by which all things are formed, and transformed. Transformation is the process by which something changes from one state into another. *And God saw the light, that it was good: and God divided the light from the darkness.* Through God's forming of light, darkness could be seen, the light separating us from darkness, physically as well as spiritually. God's thought, idea or concept of heaven is that it would consist of light and darkness. But God did not form darkness or evil. He created the idea or concept of darkness and evil to give man free will, the freedom to choose for his self.

I form the light, and create darkness: I make peace, and create evil: I the Lord do all these things. Isaiah 45:7

Man chose to form darkness and evil through his own creation and mistakenly call it good (Isaiah 5:20). Without spiritual light, man remains in darkness, a spiritual darkness formed by his own word. What differentiates a thought from a word is the greater degree of energy required to take it from a thought to a word or belief, which is emotion. It is emotion that motivates us to perform a work, to take some action.

And God said, Let there be a firmament in the midst of the waters, and let it divide the waters from the waters. And God made the firmament, and divided the waters that were under the firmament from the waters that were above the firmament; and it was so. And God called the firmament Heaven. Genesis 1:6-8

Light has been made, formed through God's word; through His works. God would then make a firmament, a place in which the light could be contained. He called this firmament *Heaven*. The word *firmament* means *an expanse,* this heaven or firmament symbolizing *our mind,* where an expansion of thought takes place. This firmament, like the mind, divides the waters under the firmament from the waters above the firmament; the *waters* symbolizing the *thoughts of our mind.* The waters *above the firmament* symbolize *our higher thoughts,* which are positive and constructive, while the waters *below the firmament* symbolize *our lower thoughts,* those that are negative and destructive. The mind has the ability to divide these higher and lower thoughts.

And God said, Let the waters under the heaven be gathered together unto one place, and let the dry land appear, and it was so. And God called the dry land Earth; and the gathering together of the waters called he Seas: and God saw that it was good. Genesis 1:9,10

Man, through an unholy spirit, has brought about a concentration of these negative thoughts within himself. To stop their destructive effects, he must follow the pattern given in God's creation process. He must gather these lower waters called *Seas* into one place. As God's Spirit moved upon the face of the waters, man's holy spirit, if not resisted, will move upon these well-hidden negatively charged thoughts or memories, bringing them up to the surface, into our awareness. When these lower waters, hidden in the darkness of denial or repression, are brought up into the light of the conscious mind, we see what lies beneath them, in the *Earth,* symbolizing the *Heart.*

And God said, Let the earth bring forth grass, and herb yielding seed, and the fruit tree yielding fruit after its kind, whose seed is in itself, upon the earth; and it was so. Genesis 1:11

As the *heaven* brings forth waters, the *mind* brings forth thoughts. But it is the *earth* that contains seed, and it is the seed of the earth that brings forth, as seen in the word *grass,* meaning *to sprout, to bring forth.* We call a thought a seed, but it is not seed until it is sown, the word *seed* meaning *something sown.* Seed is sown in the earth, not in the heaven; in the heart, not in the mind. A thought becomes a seed, word, or belief the moment it is seeded; accepted into the heart through emotional energy. A thought, being mental energy, does not contain the power needed for the thought to become a reality, just as a seed, carried through the heaven by the wind, does not have the power to bring forth until it intercourses with the earth. If the seed sown in the heart is evil, it cannot be eliminated by good thoughts. That which was sown in the heart through painful emotions will remain evil; as negative and destructive energy, until it is transformed into positive and constructive or creative energy. These evil seeds are being nourished continually by the lower waters; by the negatively charged thoughts buried so deep within the psyche that most of us are still unaware of their existence. Whatever thoughts we accepted into our heart through the power of emotion, became the seeds that in the process of time brought forth, becoming our reality. Whatever type of seed we sow, be it good or evil, positive or negative, will produce fruit after its own kind.

Now the parable is this: The seed is the word of God. Luke 8:11

The good seed or word, truth, manifests as light, and is constructive. The evil seed or word, a lie, manifests as darkness, and is destructive.

And the earth brought forth grass, and herb yielding seed after his kind, and the tree yielding fruit, whose seed is in itself, after his kind: and God saw that it was good. And the evening and the morning were the third day. Genesis 1:12,13

Grass seed, herb seed, and the tree yielding fruit, all good seed producing good fruit, *and God saw that it was good.* God did not make evil seed. He created the possibility for it to be made through free will. The *thorns and thistles* that came into existence in the garden were the result of man's choice to eat of the fruit in the midst of the garden.

And unto Adam he said, Because thou hast hearkened unto the voice of thy wife, and hast eaten of the tree, which I commanded thee, saying, Thou shalt not eat of it: cursed is the ground for thy sake; in sorrow shalt thou eat of it all the days of thy life; Thorns and thistle shall it bring forth to thee; ... Genesis 3:17,18

Eating of the fruit in the midst of the garden is accepting the false word or belief as truth, the lie being sown in our heart, which brings with it, sorrow. The *thorns and thistles* symbolize the *pain and aggravation* we bring into our life because we accepted these lies as truth.

For the invisible things of him from the creation of the world are clearly seen, being understood by the things that are made, even his eternal power and Godhead; so they are without excuse ... Romans 1:20

The *invisible* or spiritual things of God are seen through God's creation, made through His word. Everything that God made was good. If everything in our life was not good, we can determine that we have formed a creation through our own word, one that was not good.

The Godhead

And God said, Let us make man in our image, after our likeness:..
Genesis 1:26

The *Godhead* refers to God's image: God, His word, and His Spirit. Man is made after God's likeness. Man sows his seed by his energy into the mother, as God sowed His word by His Spirit into the earth. The invisible or spiritual aspect of the Godhead reveals that as gods, being made in the image of God, we have a seed that cannot be seen, sown through an energy that cannot be measured. The spiritual creation process begins when a thought is created in our mind. If we continue to concentrate on that thought, we lend a degree of energy to it, but not enough to bring it into existence. It is only through the greater degree of emotional energy that our heart opens up to receive the energized thought, which now sown, becomes a seed, word, or belief. The creation process is complete when our word, through the power of our actions, becomes our reality.

Jesus answered them, Is it not written in your law, I SAID, YE ARE GODS? If he called them gods, unto whom the word of God came...
John 10:34

The problem arises when our creation does not match God's creation; when we have a thought that is not good, not the truth. The problem is compounded when the untruthful thought becomes a false word or belief; an evil seed sown into our heart through an unholy spirit. When man sows his own word by his own spirit, he becomes a god in the bad sense— a false god.

So God created man in his own image, in the image of God created he him; male and female created he them. Genesis 1:27

We are all spiritually *male and female*. We are male in that we have the ability to sow spiritual seed by spiritual energy. We are female in that we serve as a protective habitat for this seed and energy. Our male aspect is our inner being of spirit and word, which is the essence of our father. Our female aspect is the receptacle for this spirit and word, which is our mother. Through a spiritual intercourse, our spiritual father sows spiritual seed through spiritual energy into our spiritual mother. The physical mother, which conceives of physical seed, is the female body. The spiritual mother, which conceives of spiritual seed, is the heart.

We are able to understand the Godhead by seeing the image of God, revealed through the creation process; the process through which things are made or brought into existence. Creation begins in the mind with a thought. A seed that will not bear fruit until it is sown into that spiritual earth called the heart through the power of emotional energy. *And the earth was without form, and void,* being without seed. *And the Spirit of God moved,* illustrating the activation of the emotional energy that will cause the thought of the mind to become a seed, word, or belief of the heart. Once conceived in the heart, through emotional, not mental, energy, it begins to form into a spiritual flesh, nourished daily by the same thought that created it. In the process of time, through actions that demonstrate our assenting to this word or belief, we bring it into existence, be it good or evil. If our spirit and word be holy and true, it will bring forth good fruit. We will choose the right action, and the consequence of that action will be favorable. But if our spirit and word be unholy and untrue, it will produce evil fruit, causing us to take the wrong action, the consequence being unfavorable, weighing heavily upon us. Our knowledge of good and evil was taught to us. Not everything we ate of, metaphorically speaking was good; positive and constructive. Some of it was evil; negative and destructive. And we, being naive children, confused the two.

Woe unto them that call evil good, and good evil; that put darkness for light, and light for darkness… Isaiah 5:20

Woe means *grief, misery,* the consequence of calling evil good; of mistaking the darkness of a lie for the light of truth.

And no marvel; for Satan himself is transformed into an angel of light.
2 Corinthians 11:24

This is precisely what took place in the garden. In the beginning, Adam and Eve obeyed God's word. But in the process of time, they were influenced by another word, the word of the *serpent,* symbolizing *error in thought.* The lie that became the word that stood in opposition to God's word separated them from their good life in the garden. When the wrong thought became a false word or belief, their bodies were transformed, from glorified flesh to a flesh that would limit them, as we are limited by the spiritual flesh formed by our false word, which separates us from a good life.

Creation and Evolution

Creation is the process through which God brought heaven and earth into existence. Evolution is the gradual process in which something changes into a significantly different, more complex, or more sophisticated form, a process within a process. Evolution is part of the creation process. The six days of creation are arbitrary because time, as we understand it, did not exist until after Adam and Eve sinned. Heaven and earth were formed in the six days. Adam was formed after the six days— in the seventh day.

And God said, Let the earth bring forth the living creature after his kind, cattle, and creeping things, and beast of the earth after his kind: and it was so. Genesis 1:24

Prior to the seventh day formation of Adam, the first of his kind, there were the formations of the sixth day, all the living creatures of the earth, which included other human-like kinds, varying in beastly appearance, symbolizing the beastly stages in man's spiritual devolution. Adam was the first kind to be made in the image of God. Adam was the highest degree, the finest example of humankind.

The six day creation in the first book of Genesis was a physical formation. An evolutionary process; the gradual process by which the things created in God's mind were formed, each creation going through many changes before matching the image in God's mind. After this time, God entered His Sabbath, resting from the work of forming all things physical. The sabbath is an intermission between two acts, the physical act and the spiritual act. The seventh day creation in the second chapter of Genesis was the spiritual formation of Adam. The seventh day is also the day in which the spiritual transformation of man is to take place, through which he becomes *"the last Adam."*

If we add up these seven days sequentially: $1+2+3+4+5+6+7$, we get 28, which is tied to the woman's reproductive cycle, and to the cycle of the moon, which is tied to the emotions. The seventh day is a period of time in which we are given an opportunity to spiritually reproduce through the transformation of our emotional energy. These seven days play a pivotal role in understanding what has been, is, or should be taking place within us. Our legacy began when Adam and Eve disobeyed God's word, an error in judgment that subjected them to the law of sin and death, their flesh bodies, added because of sin, bringing death. The law is limitation, their flesh bodies limiting them to a lower dimension, one subject to time, which is necessary for death to occur. The fall of Adam is still going on today as mankind continues his downward spiral, a spiritual descent that's been taking place within the mind and heart of man over the past six thousand years due to his separation from God's divine attributes; a separation from God's spirit and word. Adam, the first of his kind, was the first of humankind to be formed without the necessity of a physical evolution, being formed outside of the six days. The number *six* pertains to the *physical*. The number *seven* pertains to the *spiritual*. The last Adam is being formed in the seventh day, becoming *"a quickening spirit"* (1 Corinthians 15:45).

And the Lord God formed man of the dust of the ground, and breathed into his nostrils the breath of life; and man became a living soul. Genesis 2:7

Adam was formed out of the dust of the earth in the seventh day, made a spiritual being, made in the image of God. The *dust* symbolizes *inactivity,* Adam inactive with respect to the divine attributes of God prior to his formation. The last Adam, inactive with respect to the spirit and word of God, will be transformed from this spiritual inactivity in the seventh day; in the seventh thousandth year from the fall of the first Adam, which began with the new millennium. Adam, who once had the ability to experience the physical and spiritual realms simultaneously, forfeited this ability by choosing to accept a belief that formed the flesh that limited him, making him subject to death, and to the process of evolution, which for his descendants, became a devolution, as man becomes more and more beastly from within, which he demonstrates through his increasing beastly behavior. The varying stages of beastly man who walked upon the face of the earth represent levels or degrees of existence, existing below God's perfect creation of the human Adam. Lower than what God created us humans to be. A spiritual descent seen in the slaying of Abel, after which Cain leaves the presence of the Lord, taking a wife of the land of Nod, who are not the descendants of the higher human Adam. In slaying *Abel,* symbolizing *righteousness,* man has left the presence of God's spirit and word, taking on a beastly nature through his own spirit and word. The beastly creatures of the earth were physically formed thousands of years preceding Adam, as they have been formed spiritually, in the heart of mankind, in the thousands of years succeeding Adam. *The spirit of God* was imparted unto Adam through *the breath of life,* making him a living soul with spiritual abilities. Adam was then imparted with *the word of God,* with godly intelligence.

And the Lord God commanded the man, saying, Of every tree of the garden thou mayest freely eat: But of the tree of the knowledge of good and evil, thou shalt not eat of it: for in the day that thou eatest thereof thou shalt surely die. And the Lord God said, It is not good that the man should be alone; I will make him an help meet for him.

Genesis 2:17,18

Adam was made in the image of God, a spiritual being with the two divine attributes of God. Now the fourth element, the earthly female aspect, is about to be added to Adam, allowing him to interact with and enjoy the physical realm. The female aspect of Adam came through the woman, through Eve, as it is the woman that forms the flesh body in her womb. Eve provided a glorified flesh body, while Adam's portion, symbolized by his rib, provided the spiritual essence of that glorified body, which together made them divine beings, a positive transformation that allowed them to enjoy the pleasures of the five senses. Adam and Eve were now experiencing the best of both a spiritual and physical existence. This was the greatest gift God could impart to His perfect human. The word *Eve* means *life-giver,* that life being a physical existence, experienced and enjoyed through their glorified bodies. Adam and Eve were placed in the Garden of Eden. The word *garden* means *protection.* The word *Eden* means *pleasure, to live voluptuously* (consisting of, or characterized by strong visual and tactile delights; devoted to, or frequently indulging in, sensual gratification). With Eve came a life full of visual and tactile delights. However, with it also came a *dangerous arrogance,* symbolized by Esau's *red pottage,* which he forfeited his birthright for. They began to entertain the thought of being equal with God, which would be the beginning of their downfall. The very spiritual book of Job depicts this nature in man, showing his rise and fall. Job and his wife, like Adam and Eve, have been given everything. But soon all is lost. What does Job take from his lesson? That being righteous does not make one equal with God. It does not make one God. Job learns that he is not nearly as powerful or as righteous as he thought he was.

Where wast thou when I laid the foundations of the earth? declare, if thou hast understanding. Who hath laid the measures thereof, if thou knowest? or who hath stretched the line upon it? Whereupon are the foundations thereof fastened? or who laid the corner stone thereof; When the morning stars sang together, and all the sons of God shouted for joy? Or who shut up the sea with doors, when it brake forth, as if it had issued out of the womb?
Job 38:4-8

Adam and Eve are about to forfeit their voluptuous life in the garden. Adam has been given instruction, which he has passed on to Eve. They are not to eat of the tree in the midst of the garden, the tree of the knowledge of good and evil. They have already eaten of the good, having a positive experience. But to eat of the good and the evil is to have the knowledge of both, to experience the negative consequence of accepting the evil, the word *serpent* meaning *to learn by experience.*

And the woman said unto the serpent, We may eat of the fruit of the trees of the garden: But the fruit of the tree which is in the midst of the garden, God hath said, Ye shall not eat of it, neither shall ye touch it, lest ye die. And the serpent said unto the woman, Ye shall not surely die. For God doth know that in the day that ye eat thereof, then your eyes shall be opened, and ye shall be as gods, knowing good and evil.
Genesis 3:2-5.

The *serpent* symbolizes the *lie;* any thought that opposes God's word, which is truth. The *woman* is the receptacle for the lie, which is the *mind*. Eating of the fruit of the tree in the midst of the garden is accepting thoughts that are not the truth into our heart. These lies are tempting because they are mixed with truth, the knowledge of good and evil. That's the subtlety. The truth is, they were already gods, made in the image of God. And eating of the evil would in fact make them gods, false gods. The lie was that they would not die if they ate of the evil; the sin that formed the physical flesh that brings death. Adam and Eve are about to exercise their free will, having the ability to choose between two opposing thoughts. God's word, which is truth, was no longer the only word. The serpent's word, a lie, forms the sinful flesh that is the carnal mind. *"For to be carnally minded is death."*

For my thoughts are not your thoughts, neither are your ways my ways, saith the Lord. For as the heavens are higher than the earth, so are my ways higher than your ways, and my thoughts than your thoughts.
Isaiah 55:8,9

The physical act that caused Adam and Eve to commit sin was preceded by the spiritual act that causes us to commit sin. That act is intercourse, the spiritual equivalent of which is communication. What was once a sacred union between the mind and heart (female) and the inner being of pure spirit and pure truth (male) became unclean. Adam and Eve had accepted a belief that would have them emulating the beasts, bringing upon themselves a beastly lust that could not be tempered, the physical revealing the spiritual.

Because that, when they knew God, they glorified him not as God, neither were thankful; but became vain in their imaginations, and their foolish heart was darkened. Professing themselves to be wise, they became fools, And changed the glory of the incorruptible God into an image made like to corruptible man, and to birds, and fourfooted beasts, and creeping things. Wherefore God also gave them up to uncleanness through the lusts of their own hearts, to dishonor their own bodies between themselves. Who changed the truth of God into a lie, and worshipped and served the creature more than the Creator, who is blessed for ever. Amen. Romans 1:21-25

Adam and Eve made the choice to disregard the word of God and listen to their own vain thoughts, which drove them from the garden, separating them from their voluptuous life. They were no longer able to enjoy the pleasures the garden had to offer because of the state of their mind and heart. They were no longer dwelling in a pure spiritual state. They had become unclean, corrupted. And their bodies, through the erroneous word or belief they accepted into their hearts, were transformed from glorified flesh to corruptible flesh, likened to *corruptible man,* four footed beasts, and creeping things, which grounded them to the physical realm, where they were subject to the limitations of the third dimension, and consequently, to death.

Unto Adam also and to his wife did the Lord God make coats of skins, and clothed them. Genesis 3:21

These *coats of skin,* hairy flesh, characterizing the beastly word they accepted into their hearts, took the place of their glorified bodies. And in place of the aprons they used to hide their shame, a preponderance of hair, pointing to the origin of the sin that brought their shame, an unholy intercourse; a negative and destructive communication with the mind and heart. Additional hair was added to absorb the sweat that accumulated as they labored to bring forth the good fruit of the earth, which prior to their error or sin was effortless, having no *"thorns and thistles,"* no evil seed. Pain was added to childbirth, representing the emotional pain we will experience as we labor to enter back into the joyous life we had before we accepted these evil seeds; this false word of false beliefs, into our heart. We have no choice but to enter this world with a physical flesh body. That was the consequence of accepting the lie or *iniquity* in the garden, which forms the robe of sinful flesh. And we can do nothing to change the fact that we were conceived in *sin,* as man lusts for woman and woman lusts for man, a natural desire inherent to this flesh body. Lust is sin.

Behold, I was shapen in iniquity; and in sin did my mother conceive me.
Psalms 51:5

We can however remove another type of flesh, along with its inherent lust or sin. This spiritual flesh, which exists inside of our physical flesh, was formed by our false word; by the lies we accepted as truth. This false word is darkness, which we have mistaken for the light of truth, mistaking evil for good, which comes with sorrowful consequences. We have separated ourselves from a life of joy, removing our ability to fully enjoy our life by replacing God's good spirit and word with an evil spirit and word. Our word consists of every evil seed or false belief we accepted into our heart throughout our life, forming layer upon layer upon layer of sinful flesh over our heart, a spiritual foreskin that can only be removed through a spiritual circumcision. *"Circumcise yourselves to the Lord, and take away the foreskins of your heart"* (Jeremiah 4:4).

The Godhead as seen through Elohim and the Patriarchs

The Hebrew name for God is *ELOHIM,* which when divided into three sections reveals the image of God.

EL = God the Father (*Abraham*): *Father Abraham.*
OH = Son, Seed, Word (*Isaac*): *in Isaac shall the seed be called.*
IM = Holy Spirit, Energy, Power (*Jacob*): *the mighty God of Jacob.*

We see the *IM* with Moses at the burning bush, where God instructs him to return to Egypt and retrieve the children of Israel out of bondage. Moses asks God, *"Who shall I say sent me?"* God replies, *"Tell them I AM hath sent me unto you,"* the *I AM* being the *IM* in *EL-OH-IM,* the *Holy Spirit* of God, which *Moses* symbolizes, his *staff* or *rod* symbolizing the *power* of the Holy Spirit. When the children of Israel cried out, the Spirit was there to retrieve them out of bondage. Having a strong desire to change our life is crying out from our heart, activating the holy spirit, whose divine purpose is to retrieve us out of spiritual bondage, out from under the law of limitation we impose upon ourselves by believing the lies.

The Three Eras

The patriarchs Abraham, Isaac, and Jacob also show us three eras. The Father era of Abraham, which began four thousand years ago, the Son-ship era of Isaac, which began two thousand years ago, and the Holy Spirit era of Jacob, which began in the year 2000. Each era associated with one of the three groups that God has dealt with: Abraham with Israel, Isaac with Judah, and Jacob with Zion. As we complete the era of Isaac, completing the sixth day; six thousand years in which God has worked with descendants of the fallen human, we enter God's seventh day, entering the third and final era of Jacob or era of Spirit, in which God enters His rest. It is time for us to awaken out of what the Bible calls *"the spirit of slumber,"* and be moved by the holy spirit to begin our spiritual works. According to the Gregorian calendar, we are at the beginning of the *third day*.

And on the third day there was a marriage feast in Cana of Galilee... Now six stone waterjars were there, placed according to the Jewish custom of purification, each containing two or three measures. Jesus says to them, "Fill the jars with water." And they filled them to the top. And he says to them, "Draw now, and carry to the ruler of the feast." And they carried some. And when the ruler of the feast tasted the water made wine, and knew not whence it was, (but those servants knew who had drawn the water,) the ruler of the feast called the bridegroom.
John 2:6-9

The *six stone waterjars* symbolize *six thousand years filled with stonehearted people*. But those that are drawn out of the *water,* symbolizing *iniquity*, will, through the power of truth, be made *wine,* symbolizing *spirit*. As we enter the third day, it is time for a spiritual marriage to take place, the word *marriage* meaning *intimate relationship, intercourse*. It is time for the good seed or word of truth to intercourse with our heart, which takes place through the holy spirit of our heart, lying dormant until activated by a strong desire to be healed. It is through the good seed or word of truth that the holy spirit is revitalized, restored to the state in which we received it at birth. God caused no water to fall on the ground until after the six days. The rain, symbolizing the outpouring of the spirit, is held up until the seventh day. As God enters His rest in this seventh day, His spirit is being poured out for one divine purpose— to sow the word of truth in our heart, as the good seed was sown in the earth on the third day.

And it shall come to pass in the last days, saith the Lord, that I will pour out of my spirit upon all flesh... Acts 2:17

... one day is with the Lord as a thousand years, and a thousand years as one day. 2 Peter 3:8

It is the beginning of the third and seventh day.

It is the beginning of the seventh day; the beginning of the seventh thousandth year since the first Adam rejected the word of God in the garden, bringing error or sin. It is also the beginning of the third day; the beginning of the third thousandth year since the word of God, delivered to the world through the second Adam, was rejected. The second Adam was Jesus, God's word or seed made flesh. Jesus symbolizes truth, which takes away sin, removing the error in our thoughts and beliefs. It was in the seventh day that the first Adam was formed, and in which *the last Adam* will be transformed. It is time for a new creation to be formed within us, which takes place by following God's creation process. It is a spiritual creation; that of *"a new heaven and a new earth,"* symbolizing *a new mind and a new heart* (Revelation 21:1).

And so it is written, The first Adam was made a living soul; ... the last Adam was made a quickening spirit. 1 Corinthians 15:45

The word *quickening* means *to (re-)vitalize, make alive, give life.* The dictionary meaning of revitalize is to impart new life or vigor to; to restore the vitality of. As man enters the third day, he is given one last opportunity to revitalize his holy spirit through the conception of truth within his heart.

The third day:

The day the good seed was sown in the earth.
The day the word of God is to be sown in the heart.
The day the water is to be turned into wine.

Let's take a look at this third day with the children of Israel.

Chapter Two
Israel

Before we take a look at this third day, let's look at man's processing. He begins in the garden, made in the image of God, partaking of both a spiritual and physical existence. But he forfeits this existence when he accepts a belief that is not the truth, separating himself from God's spiritual essence, and consequently from the garden. It was to be only the beginning of man's spiritual descent, culminating in the flood that would carry Noah, who embodied the spiritual essence of God, to safety. Abraham would be the next preserver of God's righteousness, followed by Joseph, who illustrates the preservation of God's word in Egypt by storing up the corn that will feed the people during the famine, which is all over the face of the earth.

Behold, the days come, saith the Lord God, that I will send a famine in the land, not a famine of bread, nor a thirst for water, but of hearing the words of the Lord: ... Amos 8:11

Egypt symbolizes the *World*, the *corn* symbolizing the *spiritual word of God*, the word *ear* meaning *to hear*. The world is starving for spiritual truth. One eats of the *corn* by hearing (obeying) the spiritual word of God. The children of Israel, who entered Egypt during the famine, were free as long as they were ruled by Joseph and the kings that knew Joseph. But when they die out, and a king arises that does not know Joseph, the children go into bondage. When God's word of truth dies or is forgotten, the people go into bondage. Moses was the next one chosen to preserve the word of God.

Drawn out of the water as a child, he is taken to a land where his life was preserved.

> ... *And she called his name Moses: and she said, Because I drew him out of the water.* Exodus 2:10

Now the children of Israel are about to be drawn out of the *water,* symbolizing the *waste* that made them subject to the bondage of Egypt, and taken to the Promised Land, where they will be given an opportunity to preserve their lives.

Moses' Journey

Moses' journey begins when he slays the Egyptian, at which time he leaves Egypt, and comes to Midian where he sits down at a well. The word *Midian* means *brawling, contentious, discord, and strife*, describing the controversy between Moses and the Egyptian, between the spirit and the bondage of the flesh. We must fight against the part of ourselves that keeps us in bondage, fighting against our own spirit and word, through which we resurrect God's spirit and word, the two witnesses of the heart.

And their dead bodies shall lie in the street of that great city, which spiritually is called Sodom and Egypt, where also our Lord was crucified. Revelation 11:9

Through a desire to slay the Egyptian part of ourselves, we begin our journey towards freedom. The *well,* where Moses drew water, symbolizes the *deep understanding* we draw from throughout our spiritual journey. Moses drew this water for the seven daughters of Midian, watering the flock. The word *daughter* means *to build, begin to build (-er), make repair, obtain children.* The word *seven* means *to be complete, to be perfected.* To be watered is to be given something to drink, something to think about. The spirit influences the thoughts of our mind, giving us the power *to think differently,* which is *repentance.* With a new way of thinking, we can begin to build upon this foundation of truthful thoughts, ultimately repairing the damage that has been done to our spiritual house of the Lord or temple, which is the heart. Moses is given *Zipporah,* meaning *to skip about, i.e. to return.* Moses will soon be instructed to return to Egypt and retrieve the children of Israel, leading them to mount Sinai, as he led the flock of the seven daughters to Mount Horeb, another name for mount Sinai. The root meaning of *Sinai* is *desolate, to slay, be dried up,* describing the desert, and a necessary spiritual state. Like the children of Israel, we have an opportunity to do what Moses has done, which is to slay the part of ourselves that keeps us in bondage by becoming desolate or void of the negative and destructive energy behind the addiction that causes our limitations, preventing us from doing what we want to do in life, and from receiving what we want out of life. *Egypt* symbolizes the *World,* which can be a place of freedom and protection as it was for Joseph, Moses, and Jesus. Or a place of bondage and hopelessness as it was for the children of Israel. If we are drawn out of the waste in our life, as Moses was drawn out of the water, living in the world will be a blessing. But if we fear confronting the enemy within, the world becomes a curse, as we will remain enslaved, bound by the error that is responsible for our current reality.

Adam and Eve took pleasure in their life in the garden. It was only after accepting the word of error into their heart that they were separated from the good life. To turn our sorrow into joy, we must begin the *spiritual process* symbolized by the *seven daughters* of Midian; a process that makes us free, allowing us to enjoy the pleasures of this world without the bondage, the burden that is caused by our own word (Jeremiah 23:36). Through this christ healing process we resurrect the two witnesses of the heart: God's spirit and word; love and truth.

And after three days and a half the Spirit of life from God entered into them, and they stood upon their feet; and great fear fell upon them which saw them. Revelation 11:11

This resurrection takes place after *three and a half days;* after thirty-five hundred years. It's been thirty-five hundred years since Moses retrieved the children of Israel out from the bondage of Egypt. Now it's our turn to be taken out from the spiritual bondage caused by the spiritual flesh formed by our own word. This is made possible through the help of our two internal witnesses. Physical manifestations of these two witnesses were Moses and Aaron, Joshua and Caleb, Elijah and Elisha, and John the Baptist and Jesus. It is time to be led into a better land, into a better life, in which we are free, illustrated through the journey of the children of Israel, God's chosen people, chosen to teach us about ourselves!

Israel's Journey

And it came to pass in the process of time, that the king of Egypt died: and the children of Israel sighed by reason of the bondage, and they cried, and their cry came up unto God by reason of the bondage. Exodus 2:23

When we have a strong desire to change our life, we are crying out, activating the first covenant, *Ishmael,* meaning *God will hear.*

For it is written, that Abraham had two sons, the one by a bondmaid, the other by a freewoman... which things are an allegory: for these are the two covenants... Galatians 4:22,24

God's covenant or agreement with us is that if we cry out, He will hear us, as He said to Moses, *"tell the children* (whose cry came up before God) *I AM hath sent you,"* I AM meaning *I WILL BE THERE.* When we cry out, the holy spirit of our heart will be there to lead us out of the negative aspect of Egypt, out of the bondage or limitation caused by the flesh. The children of Israel have activated the Spirit, which Moses symbolizes, by crying out from their heart. The same Spirit that moved upon the waters in the beginning of creation is now moving upon the waters of the Red Sea, dividing it to expose the *ground* that will bring them salvation.

And Moses said unto the people, Fear ye not, stand still and see the salvation of the Lord... But lift thou up thy rod, and stretch out thine hand over the sea, and divide it: and the children of Israel shall go on dry ground through the midst of the sea. Exodus 14:13,16

The word *still* means *be silent, quiet self,* the *rod* symbolizing the *power of the holy spirit,* which is lifted up when we quiet our mind, bringing *the waters under the firmament,* symbolizing *the thoughts and memories hidden in the mind,* into our awareness, exposing the *ground,* revealing their source. *And God called the dry ground Earth.* When the negative and destructive thoughts that have been hidden in the depths of our mind are brought up, into the conscious mind, we discover the source of this evil, which is in the *Earth,* symbolizing the *Heart,* the subconscious. We must pass through these waters, as the children of Israel passed through the Red Sea, which is to be made aware of these lower thoughts. We cannot change or transform what is in darkness, what we do not see. Transformation requires light, the light of awareness. And it is our holy spirit that brings us into this light.

We activate the holy spirit of our heart through our strong desire to change our life, starting the process that will bring us out of bondage, out of spiritual and physical addiction, out from under the law of limitation imposed by our word of error, which forms the flesh that fights against the holy spirit.

And Israel saw that great work which the Lord did upon the Egyptians: and the people feared the Lord, and believed the Lord, and his servant Moses. Exodus 14:31

This initial transition is a *great work* of the Lord, made possible through the Spirit, which Moses symbolizes. The mind will fear the power that made this transition possible, which is to respect it. The children give reverence to this power, their fear being holy. But once this external source of power pulls back, so the children can begin the process of revitalizing their own internal holy spirit through their own works, the fear quickly becomes unholy.

... and they were sore afraid: and the children of Israel cried out unto the Lord. And they said unto Moses, Because there were no graves in Egypt, hast thou taken us away to die in the wilderness? wherefore hast thou dealt with us, to carry us forth out of Egypt? Exodus 14:10,11

No longer mindful of the great power that retrieved them, they become doubtful, losing the trust they needed to carry them through this rough place called the wilderness, their minds overcome with fear, reverting to the same unholy spirit that kept them in bondage. The six stations in the wilderness are representative of our six metaphorical days of spiritual works, which would have allowed them to enter into the Promised Land and take their rest. But they rebelled, journeying from the Red Sea to *Shur,* meaning *to turn, travel about as a harlot or merchant,* illustrating the inclination to sell ourselves on the same false images or beliefs we should be battling to overcome. They were sure that God had brought them into the wilderness to die. The unholy spirit that gave life to this lie was fear. With fear and doubt consuming their minds, they had nothing good to think; nothing good to drink for *three days,* representing the *three thousand years* that man has been separated from his spiritual essence of holy spirit and seed, which lay buried deep within his *heart.*

For as Jonas was three days and three nights in the whale's belly; so shall the Son of man be three days and three nights in the heart of the earth. Matthew 12:40

When the children of Israel come to *Marah* they find water, but are not able to drink of it because it's *bitter,* the meaning of the word *Marah*. We find this bitterness symbolized in the Passover meal, which they ate with *bitter herbs*. Passing over from our old way of life into a new way of life will not be easy. But it will be worth it. We have got to trust God by trusting in our holy spirit during this difficult time. We must not allow ourselves to become fearful and doubtful about leaving our old unprofitable way of life. If we hang in there and make it through the initial fear, doubt, and bitterness, we will gain strength at the next station in our journey.

And they came to Elim, where were twelve wells of water, and threescore and ten palm trees: and they encamped there by the waters.
Exodus 15:27.

Elim means *strength,* the number *twelve* representing *judgment,* which begins with the thoughts of our mind and concludes with the beliefs of our heart, through which we gain strength. The seventy palm trees represent the period of time in which these changes in our mind and heart take place. This transformation will result in us becoming a spiritual *palm,* meaning *to be erect,* a purification process that brings an end to our sin, reconciles our spiritual debt, and brings in everlasting righteousness (Daniel 9:24). But the children of Israel did not take advantage of this great opportunity, making their way to the wilderness of Sin, where once again they murmur against God, and against His servants, Moses and Aaron. Yet God continued to help them, giving them manna for *bread* and *quail* for meat, just what they needed *to overcome* their spiritual *sluggishness.* But the manna intended to free them came to symbolize the law that kept them in bondage. They would eat of this manna, remaining under the carnal law, for forty years, until their children made the transition from the wilderness to the Promised Land. From the wilderness of Sin they make their way to *Rephidim,* which means *to spread (as a bed), to refresh:–comfort.* Again, there is no water to drink. And again, they murmur against Moses.

> ....*Wherefore is this that thou hast brought us up out of Egypt, to kill us and our children and our cattle with thirst? And Moses cried unto the Lord, saying, What shall I do unto this people? They be almost ready to stone me.* Exodus 17:4

So Moses obeyed God, and did strike the rock in Horeb, and water came out. Moses called the place *Massah,* and *Meribah* because of the *chiding* of the children of Israel. And because they *tempted* the Lord saying, *"is the Lord among us, or not?"* We are to trust in God by trusting in our spirit from God as we go through this process. Our holy spirit will not let us down. This rough place is to prove us, to see if we are willing to fight the fear of surrendering the control of our old way of life in order to have a new and better way of life. Israel went on to fight Amalek, a descendant of Esau, illustrating the battle we must fight against the stubborn and arrogant part of ourselves that would have us forfeiting our right to a new life, as Esau forfeited his birthright for a mess of *red pottage,* which translates to *dangerous arrogance* (Genesis 25:30-34). The children of Israel move on from Rephidim and make their way to the wilderness of Sinai, the final stop in their journey. It is here that they are to prepare for the *third day.*

> *On the third New-Moon after the going-out of the Children of Israel from the land of Egypt, on the (very) day they came to the Wilderness of Sinai. They moved on from Refidim and came to the Wilderness of Sinai, and encamped in the wilderness. There Israel encamped, opposite the mountain. Now Moshe went up to God, and YHWH called out to him from the mountain, saying: Say thus to the house of Yaakov (Jacob)*

yes, tell the Children of Israel: You yourselves have seen what I did to Egypt, how I bore you on eagle's wings and brought you to me. So now, if you will hearken, yes, hearken to my voice and keep my covenant, you shall be to me a special-treasure from among all peoples. Indeed, all the earth is mine, but you, you shall be to me a kingdom of priests, a holy nation. These are the words that you are to speak to the Children of Israel. Moshe came, and had the elders of the people called, and set before them these words, with which YHWH had commanded him. And all the people answered together, they said: All that YHWH has spoken, we will do. And Moshe reported the words of the people to YHWH. YHWH said to Moshe: Here, I am coming to you in a thick cloud, so that the people may hear when I speak with you, and also that they may have trust in you for ever. And Moshe told the words of the people to YHWH. YHWH said to Moshe: Go to the people, make them holy, today and tomorrow, let them scrub their clothes, that they may be ready for the third day, for on the third day YHWH will come down before the eyes of all the people, upon Mount Sinai.
Exodus 19:1-11 (The Five Books of Moses)

As the children of Israel came to this third day, so too have we. A day in which something most holy is to take place. The holy thing that is to take place is the sowing of God's holy seed, a marriage, like that of Cana of Galilee; a spiritual intercourse between God and His bride Israel. At the sound of the shofar, the children of Israel are to ascend the mount.

Now it was on the third day, when it was daybreak: There were thunder-sounds, and lightning, a heavy cloud on the mountain, and an exceedingly strong shofar sound. And all the people in the camp trembled. Exodus 19:16 (The Five Books of Moses)

But the children of Israel could not ascend the mount because of fear. They were afraid of this new experience, desiring to return to their old life, to what they knew and had grown comfortable with. They chose to remain in their old life instead of stepping out in faith and discover a new life. With a desire to return to the bondage of Egypt, they are given the Ten Commandments, the spirit of which has already been broken, Moses illustrating their breaking of the word or letter as he came down off the mount.

And Moses said unto the people, Fear not: for God is come to prove you, and that his fear may be before your faces, that ye sin not. And the people stood afar off, and Moses drew near unto the thick darkness where God was. And the Lord said unto Moses, Thus thou shalt say unto the children of Israel, Ye have seen that I have talked with you from heaven. Ye shall not make with me gods of silver, neither shall ye make unto you gods of gold. An altar of the earth thou shalt make unto me... Exodus 20:20-24

God dwells in *darkness* to us as long as we resist the spirit of God, which brings us light. If we continue to resist the spiritual energy that brings awareness to our hidden thoughts and feelings, we will never understand the circumstances of our life, never understanding what has brought us to the uncertain place in which we now find ourselves. God speaks to us from *heaven;* from our *mind.* But it is the *earth*, symbolizing our *heart* that serves as the altar, where we are to offer up spiritual sacrifices. *"The sacrifices of God are a broken spirit... and a contrite heart"* (Psalms 51:17). Israel never ascended the mount. They remained at the bottom of the mount worshipping the *gold calf,* symbolizing the *false image or belief* that keeps us in physical and spiritual bondage.

When the children of Israel entered Egypt, whose time differs from ours by a factor of 10 to 1, they remained free for the first *forty years,* as we remain free for the first *four years* after we enter the World, after which time we began replacing love with fear and truth with lies as a result of the negative things we saw, heard, felt, and experienced. This fear, along with lies or *iniquity,* will rule us for approximately *thirty-nine years,* illustrated by the children of Israel, who spent *three hundred and ninety years* in bondage. After four hundred and thirty years, they began a journey that should have led them to freedom.

Lie also upon thy left side, and lay the iniquity of the house of Israel upon it: according to the number of the days that thou shalt lie upon it thou shalt bear the iniquity... according to the number of the days, three hundred and ninety days: so shall thou bear the iniquity of the house of Israel. Ezekiel 4:4,5

After forty-three years, many of us will experience what is called a mid-life crisis. And what is in crisis is our holy spirit. If we do not take this opportunity to overcome our fears and begin the process of changing our life, we will remain in bondage, subject to the law of fear and lies or *iniquity* for the rest of our lives, as the children of Israel remained in bondage to the carnal law for *forty* years, for the rest of their lives, dying in the wilderness.

And when thou hast accomplished them, lie again on thy right side, and thou shalt bear the iniquity of the house of Judah forty days: I have appointed thee each day for a year. Ezekiel 4:6

They never experienced the joy and freedom that lay just ahead in the Promised Land, the promise of a much better life, the reward for going through the process of transforming the heart. The twelve stones placed in the Jordan symbolize the twelve steps through which our heart is transformed, making us free in every aspect of our life.

Note: The children of Israel are referred to as Judah after leaving the bondage of Egypt and passing through the Red Sea, which will be discussed in the next chapter.

When we make a heart-felt decision to move away from a way of life that has become too painful, restrictive, or unpleasant, we engage our holy spirit, making our way through a spiritual wilderness, working on the fear that has ruled our mind since childhood. With each step we take, we build trust, knowing that all we need to succeed on this journey into a new way of life has already been given into our hand, symbolizing power. Through a process activated by the mind discipline of silence, we discover the many lies that have led us into a life we do not want or no longer take pleasure in. By peeling away the layers of flesh formed by our word of false beliefs, we complete our metamorphosis, emerging from the sinful flesh that has cocooned us for so long. Emerging perfected through spiritual works, we will live joyfully in the new-found freedom that comes with a complete transformation, which is made possible through God's spirit and word.

As we conclude with Israel, we see that it was the fear of their mind that prevented them from ascending the mount, illustrating our journey through the heart. It was this fear that gave power to the lies of their mind, which formed the veil of flesh over their heart, symbolized by the veil over Moses' face, which the seed of truth, through which we are made free, could not penetrate. The children of Israel died under the bondage of the law; a law that controlled the mind and body, but did nothing to transform the heart. The way to complete freedom is through the heart; by healing the painful emotions associated with the false beliefs that keep us from feeling joy, and experiencing freedom, keeping us from the good life we inherit when we enter in and battle against the enemies of the heart.

Chapter Three
Judah

The prophet Ezekiel reveals to us that the children are referred to as Israel in Egypt and as Judah in the wilderness. The event that took place between Egypt and the wilderness, that caused their name to be changed, was their baptism in the Red Sea. Baptism is synonymous with the wedding ceremony, the bride clothed in white raiment, symbolizing her new name. Israel the bride and Moses the bridegroom, the Old Testament a type and shadow of the New Testament, Jesus the bridegroom and spiritual Israel the bride.

Moreover, brethren, I would not that ye should be ignorant, how that all our fathers were under the cloud, and all passed through the sea; And were baptized unto Moses in the cloud and in the sea;
1 Corinthians 10:1,2

In the traditional wedding ceremony, the veil is removed from the bride, symbolizing circumcision, of which there are four: two physical and two spiritual. The first circumcision takes place at a bris, when the flesh is removed from the penis. The second is upon our death, when the flesh body is separated from the soul. The two spiritual circumcisions are of the mind (eyes and ears) and of the heart. The children of Israel never experienced even their first spiritual circumcision, which would have been performed by removing the foreskin of sinful flesh formed by the lies or iniquity of their mind.

And he said, Go, tell this people, Hear ye indeed, but understand not; and see ye indeed, but perceive not. Make the heart of this people fat, and make their ears heavy, and shut their eyes; lest they see with their eyes, and hear with their ears, and understand with their heart, and convert, and be healed. Isaiah 6:9,10

The veil was never removed because they never ascended the mount on the third day, where they would have seen God. Not in the literal sense, for God is Spirit, but in the spiritual sense. They never became aware of the workings of God's spirit and word from within their mind and heart. This comes by quieting the mind, silencing the fear and lies that oppose the spirit of love and word of truth. Moses, on the other hand, saw God, lifting up his holy spirit, perfecting it through works, obeying the word of God, thereby completing his spiritual journey. Moses stood as the type and shadow bridegroom, but he also became a spiritual bride through a spiritual baptism. He was immersed by the Holy Spirit through faith, which he perfected through spiritual works, thereby immersing himself in the word of truth. When he came off the mount, he placed a *veil* over his face, illustrating Israel's *inability to perceive* of the spiritual word of God. Moses' face radiated because of the degree of energy contained in the spirit and word of God (e.g., Elisha), enough to raise the dead (2 Kings 13:21).

Now whenever Moshe would come before the presence of YHWH, to speak with him, he would remove the veil, until he had gone out; and whenever he would come out and speak to the children of Israel that which he had been commanded, the Children of Israel would see Moshe's face, that the skin of Moshe's face was radiating; but then Moshe would put back the veil on his face, until he came in to speak with him.
Exodus 34:34,35 (The Five Books of Moses)

At each spiritual circumcision, there is a spiritual passover; passing over from an old way of thinking to a new way of thinking and from an old way of feeling and believing to a new way of feeling and believing. But unfortunately the children of Israel were never able to let go of Egypt, holding on to their old way of life. And it will be unfortunate for us if we are not able to overcome the fear and lies that prevent us from letting go of the old so we can experience the new. The children of Israel died in the wilderness, never passing over into the Promised Land, never eating of the fruit of that land; the fruit of the Spirit, the result of spiritual circumcision. They never allowed their hidden thoughts and feelings to emerge, the good land, representing the good life, eluding them. Their children will now be given the same opportunity to take hold of a new way of life as the Spirit of God moves once again upon the face of the waters, as it did in the beginning of the creation of the World, and at the Red Sea.

And as they that bare the ark were come to Jordan, and the feet of the priests that bare the ark were dipped in the brim of the water, (for Jordan overfloweth all his banks all the time of harvest,) That the waters which came down from above stood and rose up upon an heap very far from the city Adam, that is beside Zaretan: and those that came down toward the sea of the plain, even the salt sea failed, and were cut off: and the people passed over right against Jericho. Joshua 3:15,16

The word *Jordan* means *to descend, to go downwards, to bring down.* Israel's children have humbled themselves before God, making their way down to the Jordan. We cannot even begin this spiritual journey until we humble ourselves to the process symbolized by the twelve stones placed in the Jordan. We must admit to ourselves that our current way is no longer working, and greatly desire a new way, at which time the *waters,* symbolizing the *erroneous thoughts,* are held back so we can make the initial transition. It is *the time of harvest;* time to separate the tares from the wheat, the lies from the truth.

And it came to pass, when all the kings of the Amorites, which were on the side of Jordan westward, and all the kings of the Canaanites, which were by the sea, heard that the Lord had dried up the waters of Jordan from before the children of Israel, until we were passed over, that their heart melted, neither was there spirit in them any more, because of the children of Israel. At that time the Lord said unto Joshua, Make thee sharp knives, and circumcise again the children of Israel the second time.
Joshua 5:1,2

Transition from Levi to Judah and from Israel to Judah

Moses gave way to Joshua, and Aaron (of the tribe of Levi) gave way to Caleb (of the tribe of Judah), the type and shadow of what was to occur fifteen hundred years later, when the letter of the law was to give way to the spirit of the law, carnal giving way to spiritual.

If therefore perfection were by the Levitical priesthood, (for under it the people received the law,) what further need was there that another priest should rise after the order of Melchisedec, and not be called after the order of Aaron? For the priesthood being changed, there is made of necessity a change also of the law... For it is evident that our Lord sprang out of Judah; of which tribe Moses spake nothing concerning priesthood.   Hebrews 7:11-14

As Israel's children pass through the Jordan River, they take on a new name through another type and shadow baptism. Their new name is *JUDAH,* and as their fathers before them, they are given an opportunity to conceive of God's holy seed, the spiritual word of God.

And the Lord said unto Joshua, This day have I rolled away the reproach of Egypt from off you. Wherefore the name of the place is called Gilgal unto this day. And the children of Israel encamped in Gilgal, and kept the passover on the fourteenth day of the month at even in the plains of Jericho. And they did eat of the old corn of the land on the morrow after the passover, unleavened cakes, and parched corn in the selfsame day. And the manna ceased on the morrow after they had eaten of the old corn of the land; neither had the children of Israel manna any more; but they did eat of the fruit of the land of Canaan that year.

Joshua 5:9-12

With a change in the priesthood, from Levi to Judah, came a change in the law. The passing of Moses was to be the passing of the Mosaic Law. They would eat no more of the *manna*, symbolizing the *carnal law*, but of the *old corn*, symbolizing the *ancient spiritual truth*.

And in that day seven women shall take hold of one man, saying, We will eat our own bread, and wear our own apparel: only let us be called by thy name, to take away our reproach. Isaiah 4:1

The *reproach* is taken away at our spiritual passover; the process of passing over from our old life of bondage to a new life of freedom, through which we receive *our own apparel;* the name of *one man,* truth, which Jesus personified. The *seven women* symbolize the *spiritual process* that changes the energy of the thoughts, feelings, and beliefs that keep us in a state of oppression, depression, and addiction; bondage. Our fear-driven thoughts, some obvious, some obscure, keep us from eating of the fruit of this new land or life that we are to become heir to. When we eat of its fruit, enjoying the aftereffect of accepting truth in our heart, we will be encouraged to complete this journey from bondage to freedom; from eating of the manna to eating of the corn; the truth that makes us free. When love and truth replace fear and lies, the law of bondage no longer exists. There will be nothing left to keep us from receiving what we truly desire.

Nevertheless what saith the scripture? Cast out the bondwoman and her son: for the son of the bondwoman shall not be heir with the son of the freewoman. So then, brethren, we are not the children of the bondwoman, but of the free. Galatians 4:30,31

The *bondwoman* symbolizes the *bondage of flesh,* an invisible flesh that can only be removed through a spiritual circumcision. *Her son,* the fruit of bondage, the *"son of perdition,"* (John 17:12), is the destruction we bring to our life and our world when we live to the lies that speak through our mind, enslaving us. When we seek the source of these unhealthy thoughts and behaviors, we have placed our feet on *holy ground.*

And he said, Draw not nigh hither: put off thy shoes from off thy feet, for the place whereon thou standest is holy ground. Exodus 3:5

And the captain of the Lord's host said unto Joshua, Loose thy shoe from off thy foot; for the place whereon thou standest is holy. And Joshua did so. Joshua 5:15

Moses and *Joshua,* symbolizing the *Spirit of God,* placed their feet on holy ground, as it is through the power of our holy spirit that we get in touch with what the *holy ground* symbolizes, which is the *heart.* As the *dry land* called *earth* brought salvation to the children of Israel, our salvation will come through our *heart.*

Fix-boundaries for the people round about, saying: Be on your watch against going up the mountain or against touching its border! Whoever touches the mountain— he is to be put-to-death, yes, death... When the (sound of the) ram's-horn is drawn out, they may go up on the mountain... Moshe went down from the mountain to the people, he made the people holy, and they washed their clothes, then he said to the people: Be ready for three days; do not approach a woman! Exodus 19:10-15
                                                                (The Five Books of Moses)

The children of Israel washed their clothes, an external act that illustrated the mental purification that would have prepared them for ascending the mount. They were to complete this mental work in the *wilderness,* symbolizing the *mind,* prior to their arriving at the mount. This would have prepared them for *touching the mount,* which illustrates *getting in touch with the heart.* The *death* associated with touching the mount represents a spiritual death, the death of the false beliefs of our heart (Revelation 3:1,2). The *fixed-boundaries* represent the *limitations of the mind,* which have prevented us from getting in touch with our heart. They were not to approach a *woman,* symbolizing the spiritual *flesh* that would prevent them from ascending the mount, which is to surmount the painful emotions of the heart. The fear and iniquity of their mind created the boundaries that kept them from discovering what was in their heart. Now their children will have an opportunity to succeed where they failed, which they illustrated by bringing down the wall that stood between themselves and the Promised Land.

Now Jericho was straitly shut up because of the children of Israel: none went out, and none came in. Joshua 6:1

Jericho symbolizes the *innermost mind,* which has been shut up because we have been afraid to confront our deepest thoughts.

And ye shall compass the city, all ye men of war, and go round about the city once. Thus shall thou do six days. And seven priests shall bear before the ark seven trumpets of ram's horns: and the seventh day ye shall compass the city seven times, and the priests shall blow with the trumpets. And it shall come to pass, that when they make a long blast with the ram's horn, and when ye hear the sound of the trumpet, all the people shall shout with a great shout; and the wall of the city shall fall down flat... Joshua 6:3-5

Compassing the city for *six days* parallels the *six stations* in the wilderness. This is the work of battling the fear and untruthful thoughts of our mind. The *seven trumpets* of ram's horns announce the onset of this *spiritual battle* of fighting against the enemies of our heart. Compassing the city *seven times* symbolizes the *spiritual process* that is to be completed in the *seventh day*, which began with the new millennium. The *wall of the city* symbolizes the *wall of the mind;* a wall of sinful flesh, whose foundation is fear and whose bricks are lies. When this wall is brought down, we see the enemies that are dwelling in our heart.

And Joshua said, Hereby ye shall know that the living God is among you, and that he will without fail drive out from before you the Canaanites, and the Hittites, and the Hivites, and the Perizzites, and the Girgashites, and the Amorites, and the Jebusites. Joshua 3:10

Beyond the wilderness is the mount. Beyond the wall of Jericho is the Promised Land. Beyond the sanctuary is the holiest place of all. Beyond the mind is the heart, in which dwell seven unholy inhabitants.

When he speaketh fair, believe him not: for there are seven abominations in his heart. Proverbs 26:25

For out of the heart proceed evil thoughts, murders, adulteries, fornications, thefts, false witness, blasphemies: Matthew 15:19

The mind is a trickster, able to conceal what is in the heart. It serves as a façade, putting on a good front, speaking its goodly words, lies. But the heart cannot be shod with such an unholy gospel without a vitriol response. It is holy ground, the holiest place of all, its unholy inhabitants designedly exposed through our mind and body; through our negative thoughts and destructive behaviors, giving us an opportunity to seek out their source, our false beliefs, the enemies of our heart, which will be cast out by way of truth as we are taken through God's healing process.

Now when Jesus was risen early the first day of the week, he appeared first to Mary Magdalene, out of whom he had cast seven devils.

Mark 16:9

If we only purify our mind through prayers, affirmations, meditations, positive thinking, and the like, neglecting to also purify our heart, we will be worse off than before because our mind will have entered a deluded state, hiding our true condition— a secret held by the heart.

When the unclean spirit is gone out of a man, he walketh through dry places, seeking rest, and findeth none. Then he said, I will return into my house from whence I came out; and when he is come, he findeth it empty, swept, and garnished. Then goeth he, and taketh seven other spirits more wicked than himself, and they enter in and dwell there: and the last state of that man is worse than the first. Even so shall it be also unto this wicked generation. Matthew 12:43-45

Changing the negative and destructive thoughts of our mind through these mind disciplines, gives us peace of mind. Believing that we have taken care of the problem, we seek *rest*, but find none. We find no rest because we have not completed our works. No matter how much we condition our mind to think a certain way, it does not change the reality of our heart. While our mind appears to be swept clean of impure thoughts, the *seven other spirits* or *spiritual impurities* of the heart remain. Our last state is worse than the first because our mind has been deluded by false peace; the veil or wall that prevents us from entering in and cleaning up our heart.

The heart, unlike the mind, has the power to manifest change that is permanent rather than temporary, eternal rather than temporal. We have become quite proficient at cleaning up the thoughts of our mind, replacing negative thoughts with positive thoughts. But these mind-words are just thoughts generated through mental energy, not containing the power needed for a complete transformation, which requires emotional energy. We must enter into our heart, into the seat of the emotions, where we will do the deeper spiritual works that removes the root of the problem, instead of just whacking the weed off at the surface; at the mind level. Purifying the mind may bring peace to our mind. It may make us feel good, and make us think we have done the works. A deception that will keep us from seeing what is still buried deep in our heart.

But be ye doers of the word, and not hearers only, deceiving your own selves. For if any be a hearer of the word, and not a doer, he is like unto a man beholding his natural face in a glass: For he beholdeth himself, and goeth his way, and straightway forgetteth what manner of man he was. James 1:22-24

Prayers and affirmations will not change the condition of man, or the world he lives in, because they do not change the heart. To manifest change that is permanent or everlasting, we must purify our heart.

Create in me a clean heart, O God; and renew a right spirit within me. Cast me not away from thy presence; and take not thy holy spirit from me. Restore unto me the joy of thy salvation; and uphold me with thy free spirit. Psalms 51:10-12

The children of Israel never touched the mount, never getting in touch with the painful emotions that empowered the false beliefs of their heart. Coming into the truth as to the true condition of our heart, is the beginning of the stage in the process that leads to complete freedom.

... Behold, a virgin shall conceive, and bear a son, and shall call his name Immanuel. Isaiah 7:14

Purification of the heart is how we become a spiritual *virgin;* a state that allows us to conceive of the truth that saves us from ourselves. The word *Immanuel* means *with us is God*. Joshua told the children of Israel that the expulsion of the seven nations from the Promised Land would be evidence that the living God was with them. Driving out these unholy inhabitants from our heart is the purification process. It revitalizes the holy spirit of love and regenerates the word of truth from within our heart. When these two divine attributes of God are restored, God is with us; when our holy spirit reaches its highest degree through its revitalization, it allows for the highest degree of conception of truth, *a son,* within that spiritual womb called the heart. Through this process, which they illustrated by compassing the city seven times (7x7), through which truth is added (49+1= 50), we celebrate our one-time spiritual Jubilee.

Jubilee, among the ancient Jews, extraordinary Sabbatical year (following every seventh ordinary Sabbatical year) celebrated every 50th year. In the year of Jubilee, the land was completely left to rest. All debts were remitted; land that had been alienated was restored to it original owners; and all Jews, who, through poverty, had obliged to hire themselves out as servants, were released from bondage. "Jubilee." Funk and Wagnalls New Encyclopedia. 1986 ed.

When we complete our six metaphorical days of spiritual works, the creation of our new heaven and earth is finished, and we enter into our rest. Our spiritual debt is paid. And the good land or life that we alienated ourselves from through hidden beliefs and unresolved thoughts and emotions, is restored to us. We will finally be free of our spiritual bondage.

The children are to take nothing out of the city of Jericho.

...Cursed be the man before the Lord, that riseth up and buildeth this city Jericho. Joshua 6:26

It is to be utterly destroyed. The word *city* means *to have your eyes opened,* and what we are to have our eyes opened to, is the evil that still exists inside of the wall of our mind; inside of the innermost or subconscious mind— inside our heart.

But the children of Israel committed a trespass in the accursed thing: for Achan, the son of Carmi, the son of Zabdi, the son of Zerah, of the tribe of Judah, took of the accursed thing: and the anger of the Lord was kindled against the children of Israel. Joshua 7:1

Judah was found guilty of taking of the *accursed thing,* as Judas, the Greek spelling of Judah, was found guilty of *iniquity,* which betrays the truth of the heart.

Now this man purchased a field with the reward of iniquity; and falling headlong, he burst asunder in the midst, and all his bowels gushed out. And it was known unto all the dwellers at Jerusalem; insomuch as that field is called in their proper tongue, Aceldama, that is to say, The field of blood. For it is written in the book of Psalms, Let his habitation be desolate, and let no man dwell therein; and his bishoprick let another take. Acts 1:18-20

The *field* symbolizes the *world,* the spirits of which have been purchased through thousands of years of iniquity. This field is called *Aceldama,* meaning *field of blood,* which translates to *world of death;* physical and spiritual death. To stop the death, we must stop the iniquity, error or sin, the wages of which is death. It was Mathias that took the place of Judas. The word *Mathias* means *gift of God.* The gift of God is His word, truth, which is to take the place of our *iniquity.*

When I saw among the spoils a goodly Babylonian garment, and two hundred shekels of silver, and a wedge of gold of fifty shekels weight, I coveted them, and took them, and they are hid in the earth in the midst of my tent, and the silver under it. Joshua 7:21

A *Babylonian garment* symbolizes a *covering of confusion.* What causes this confusion is the conflict between the truth of the heart and the lies of the mind. The silver and gold symbolize the things we covet. They are hid in the *earth* because what drives the lust is hid in the *heart*. The word *silver* means *to become pale, to fear, to be greedy*. It is the fear of our mind that undermines us, giving power to the lies that speak through our mind, which keep us from entering our heart and driving out the enemies living there. This was the *accursed thing* that kept the children of Israel from entering the Promised Land, driving out the inhabitants, and taking their inheritance. It is our mind that has been keeping us from seeing what is in our heart. By quieting our mind, we cut off the fear and iniquity of our mind, giving power to the holy spirit of our heart, which brings the light of truth, exposing the internal enemies of our heart. As each enemy of the heart is driven out, we come closer and closer to reclaiming our spiritual inheritance— the *good land* or life promised us by God. We take possession of this good life through the completion of the internal works that will result in us living in a pure spiritual, mental and emotional, state.

Take good heed therefore unto yourselves, that ye love the Lord your God. Else if ye do in any wise go back, and cleave unto the remnant of these nations, even these that remain among you, and shall make marriages with them, and go in unto them, and they to you: Know for a certainty that the Lord your God will no more drive out any of these nations from before you; but they shall be snares and traps unto you, and scourges in your sides, and thorns in your eyes, until ye perish from off this good land which the Lord God hath given you. And, behold, this day I am going the way of all the earth: and ye know in all your hearts and in all your souls, that not one thing hath failed of all the good things which the Lord your God spake concerning you; all are come to pass unto you, and not one thing faileth thereof. Therefore it shall come to pass, that as all the good things are come upon you, which the Lord your God promised you; so shall the Lord bring upon you all the evil things, until he have destroyed you from off this good land which the Lord your

God hath given you. When ye have transgressed the covenant of the Lord your God, which commanded you, and have gone and served other gods, and bowed yourselves to them; then shall the anger of the Lord be kindled against you, and ye shall perish quickly from off the good land which he hath given unto you.   Joshua 23:11-16

The Seven unholy Inhabitants of the Promised Land

Canaanite: from the primitive root meaning *to bend the knee; hence to humiliate, vanquish, bring down low, bring into subjection.* The dictionary meaning of the word humiliate is to lower the pride, dignity, or status of; to disgrace. This unholy spirit of humiliation gives life to the other six Canaanite nations.

Hittite: terror, from the primitive root meaning *to prostrate, hence to break down, either literally by violence or figuratively by confusion and fear, beat down, discourage, cause to dismay, scare, terrify; a descendant of Heth.* Heth is a son of Canaan, the fruit of humiliation; an unholy spirit that breaks us down through fear and confusion, discouraging us, terrifying us into submission, removing our self-worth, leaving us with a feeling of hopelessness.

Hivite: a villager, from the primitive root meaning *to live; by implication to declare or show; a descendant of Canaan.* This unholy spirit arises to counteract the effects of the first spirit, which has stripped us of our dignity. But descending from the same unholy spirit of humiliation, it is equally unholy. The Hivite is the spirit of self-righteousness.

Perizzite: an inhabitant of the open country, unwalled village, from an unused root meaning *to separate; a Canaanite tribe.* This unholy spirit is one of isolation, a spirit that separates one individual from another individual, or one group of people from another group of people, a spirit that keeps us from communicating with one another. Unable to bounce our thoughts off others, we are left with no mental barometer, nothing to compare what we are thinking with what others are thinking. Our mind becomes open country, where inbred thoughts are allowed to run wild, resulting in destructive thoughts and behaviors.

Girgashite: an uncertain derivative, a Canaanite tribe. This unholy spirit arises whenever we are presented with the truth. As truth begins to enter our mind, this unholy spirit immediately rises up to do battle against that truth, bringing our mind into a state of confusion. The moment of confusion is the time to fight against this unholy spirit by making a decision, and then acting on that decision. But we must act quickly because justification or support will enter in on the side of the lie, on the side of our old way of thinking, closing our window of opportunity. The goal of this unholy spirit is to keep us confused, in spiritual stagnation; from making any spiritual advancement. We must strike in the heat of this battle by making a decision on the side of the new thought. *"Do something, even if it's wrong."* Excellent advice from my teacher, which helped me in my time of confusion; a spiritual Babylon I entered a few years after his death. If it turns out we have made the wrong decision, so what, we'll get it right the next time. At least we are moving and learning; growing spiritually.

Amorite: to say, in the sense of publicity, i.e. prominence, a Canaanite tribe. This unholy spirit makes us feel as if we need to be prominent, just a little better or a little smarter than the next guy. The old expression *"wanting to be top dog"* best describes this spirit. Do we find it necessary to prove to ourselves, through internal or external verbal expression, that we are right and others are wrong? This unholy spirit is yet another by-product of centuries of humiliation, which has been passed down from generation to generation.

Jebusite: trodden, i.e. threshing place, to trample, loathe, tread (down, under [foot]), be polluted. A descendant of Canaan. We give power to this unholy spirit by failing to fight the ones that precede it, choosing unholy spirits over God's holy spirit, and our own word of lies over God's word of truth, through which we pollute God's holy name, trampling His word of truth. These unholy spirits of the heart all descend from the spirit of humiliation, all working to keep us from inheriting the spiritual promised land; the good life we acquire through the purification of our heart.

Israel, who became Judah when they crossed the Jordan and entered the Promised Land, was not to make leagues or marriages with these nations. But they disobeyed God's word. And in the end, were unable to drive them out. *Israel* and *Judah,* symbolizing the *Mind* and *Heart,* remained impure. All of us made the transition into Judah two thousand years ago when the world entered the era of Isaac; a period of mockery. We are the children of that generation, the children of Judah, and these unholy nations inhabit our heart, and subsequently our mind, manifesting in our actions. Our spiritual journey begins when we enter a spiritual Jordan, entering a humbled state of mind. No longer ruled by false peace, we bring down the wall of our mind, allowing us to see the enemies of our heart, and drive them out. These seven nations make up the evil spirit of Judah or Judas, which betrays the truth of the heart. At the root of these unholy or evil spirits, is the spirit of humiliation, which is the Canaanite, a descendant of Canaan, whose father was Ham, the progenitor of this unholy spirit. Ham, son of Noah, looked upon his father's nakedness, and was cursed because of it. *"Cursed be Canaan"* (Genesis 9:25). When we look upon the imperfections of others, we are looking upon their nakedness. But the curse comes when we fail to see our own imperfections, and work on correcting them.

And why beholdest the mote that is in thy brother's eye, but perceivest not the beam that is in thine own eye? ...Thou hypocrite, cast out first the beam out of thine own eye, and then shalt thou see clearly to pull the mote that is in thy brother's eye. Luke 6:41,42

Before we make a judgment upon someone else's behavior, we must first judge ourselves to see if we are guilty of the same behavior. And we must look closely because these behaviors manifest in different ways, beyond what we think, say and do, and into how we feel about what we are judging, which can lead us to the belief associated with those feelings. If we find that we humiliate others, we should look to see how we humiliate ourselves, which will be found in the negative way we think and feel about ourselves; in the negative words we speak about ourselves in our mind, and in the destructive ways in which we bring harm to our body. We should use our judgment of others as a mirror, as more often times than not, it is reflecting what we need to judge in ourselves. By first judging ourselves, we understand, but do not justify the negative and destructive behaviors of others, our projected judgments carrying a different spirit in that they are being judged in truth, and in spirit, which is love.

Tracing the root of humiliation

We can trace the spirit of humiliation back to Ham, but to find the spiritual root of this unholy spirit, we need look no further than religion. The spirit of humiliation has been passed down through the religious system, from generation to generation. We were told that if we did not subject ourselves to a certain belief, we were going to hell. We were told that we must be born again and saved if we wanted to escape the lake of fire, and make it into heaven. Subjecting ourselves to yet another belief would ensure that we are not left behind when the rapture takes place. These man-made religious dogmas instilled fear, and the humiliation of being told we were sinners bound for hell, made us feel inferior. The humiliation that comes with being stripped of one's self-worth had many of us accepting these doctrines as a means of reclaiming our self-worth through the unholy spirit of self-righteousness. The spirit of humiliation, working hand in hand with the spirit of fear, gave way to the anger that would resound in many a home; in words like, *"you're stupid"* or *"you'll never amount to anything,"* often extending into horrific acts of physical, emotional, and sexual abuse. Humiliation stripped us of our authentic power, leaving us with an insatiable lust for control, which many self-righteous religious devotees wielded, using the same unholy fear, feeling more and more powerful with each soul they claim to have converted or saved. If man would reclaim his authentic power, this unholy and destructive control would no longer exist, bringing unity instead of division, peace instead of war.

We find this destructive control in countries throughout the world. In religious groups willing to destroy anyone that will not submit to their way of thinking. We have evidence of this spirit of humiliation in our schools, one group targeting another group not fitting their image. This need to feel superior is the result of this evil spirit of humiliation, the spirit of Judah, which is out to destroy us all. We find this humiliating and oppressive spirit of Judah in the founding of our own country. Judah is described as an *"old lion."* The country that bears the symbol of the lion is England, from which our ancestors fled in pursuit of freedom, religious freedom at the top of the list, which can viewed in two ways: freedom of, or freedom from. When we stepped onto this new land, we were free, but our freedom from old religious practices and dogmas was short lived. We named this new land New England, but the old spirit of religious humiliation and oppression would follow after us, the old lion pulling us back into her ravenous grip, not satisfied until we once again, became prey to her religious control.

King David, who ruled over Israel and Judah, slayed the lion and the bear in his youth, the *lion* symbolizing the *unholy spirit of control*, and the lion's accomplice, the *bear*, symbolizing the *untruthful word* or *false belief*. In an attempt to make ourselves feel better about ourselves, we gave power to this destructive control, which empowers the destructive word or belief at the root of addiction, religion being a powerful addiction. This destructive spiritual energy not only destroys our relationships, but our minds and bodies through disorders, disease, and compulsions. And the country that claims the *bear* for its symbol is Russia, Stalin killing millions of his own people, like the bear, destroying much flesh. As we enter the spiritual era of Jacob, which is grouped with Zion, the city of David, we are youths. And like David, we must fight against the lion; the unholy and unhealthy spirit of control, a byproduct of fear. When we encounter this lion, which is to face up to it by acknowledging the area in our life in which we seek control, be it excessive or lack of control, we must also face what is behind it, which is the bear; the untruthful word or false belief, which together with the control, leads to our destructive behaviors. When the lion and the bear; the destructive spirit and word, are overcome through acknowledgment, awareness, and judgment, we will be free to enjoy the things we did before, but without the burden of addiction, the gift of purifying ourselves from the inside out.

Thou blind Pharisee, cleanse first that which is within the cup and platter that the outside of them may be clean also. Matthew 23:26

The *cup and platter* symbolize the *mind and heart*. How we think and feel determines how we act, the *outside*. By purifying our mind and heart; our thoughts and emotions, we rid ourselves of our destructive behaviors forever!

The children of Israel served the Lord all the days of Joshua, and all the days of the elders that outlived Joshua, as their ancestors served the Lord, living in freedom, all the days of Joseph and all the days of the kings that knew Joseph. A *king* symbolizes a *spirit,* be it good or evil, positive or negative.

When we resisted our holy spirit, it allowed for spirits not associated with the word of truth to enter in. These unholy spirits had intercourse, communicated, with the heart, which the children of Israel illustrated by making marriages with the Canaanite nations, which God commanded them not to do. This led them back under the bondage of the law, which they had briefly been taken out from under. If we use the power of our mind to stop our destructive behaviors, but fail to purify our heart, we will continue to be influenced by the negative and destructive energies or unholy spirits of our heart on a subconscious level, leading us back into bondage, causing us to return to our old addiction, or replacing it with a new one.

For it had been better for them not to have known the way of righteousness, than, after they have known it, to turn from the holy commandment delivered unto them. But it has happened unto them according to the true proverb, THE DOG IS TURNED TO HIS OWN VOMIT AGAIN; *and the sow that was washed to her wallowing in the mire. 2 Peter 2:21,22*

The book of Judges, which follows the book of Joshua, teaches us that we raise up judges, our own judgment, when we forfeit our inherent good to make room for the evil, which the children of Israel illustrated by cohabiting with the seven nations inhabiting the Promised Land. These judges came to deliver *Israel* and *Judah* out of the hands of those that spoiled them, as external judgments, troubles in our life, come to deliver our *Mind* and *Heart* from the power of the unholy spirits that pollute them. But they would not hearken to their judges, as man does not hearken to the judgment coming upon the earth, and upon his earthly body, in the form of destruction, and disease; signs not seen by the generation Jesus called *adulterous*.

And I saw, when for all the causes whereby backsliding Israel committed adultery I had put her away, and given her a bill of divorce; yet her treacherous sister Judah feared not, but went and played the harlot also.
Jeremiah 3:8

"Thou shalt not commit adultery" Exodus 20:14

Adultery is taking another husband while the first husband lives. Our first husband is truth, the spiritual husband of our heart, which lives forever. We commit spiritual adultery every time a lie of our mind is communicated to our heart, a spiritual intercourse. This is precisely what Judah did when she made marriages with these Canaanite nations. She disobeyed God's word, rejecting her first love (Revelation 2:4), her first husband, truth! Judah, like Israel, played the harlot by making marriages with these other nations, the familiarity of which bred contempt for God's way. They demanded to be like the other nations, demanding that a king rule over them instead of God.

And the Lord said unto Samuel, Hearken unto the voice of the people, in all that they say unto thee: for they have not rejected thee, but they have rejected me, that I should not reign over them. 1 Samuel 8:7

When we first allowed the unholy spirit of fear to rule our mind, we chose *a new king*, symbolizing *a new spirit*. The king Israel chose was *Saul*, meaning *to demand*, a spirit that caused our spiritual kingdom to be taken out from under the rule of a holy spirit and word, love and truth, and turned over to an unholy spirit and word, fear and lies. It is time to turn the spiritual kingdoms of our Mind and Heart, *Israel and Judah*, over to *David*, meaning *to love*

To translate the kingdom from the house of Saul, and to set up the throne of David over Israel and over Judah… 2 Samuel 3:10

The children of Israel resisted the Spirit of God by resisting the voice of Moses in the wilderness. They continue to resist the Spirit of God by rejecting Samuel, through whom God spoke. They wanted a new king. They wanted a new spirit to rule over them. David would be the next embodiment of God's Spirit, followed by Elijah, the Spirit of whom rested upon John the Baptist, the voice of one crying out in the wilderness, preparing the children of Judah for Jesus, the word of God, spiritual truth, which came to translate the kingdom from *Saul* to *David* by teaching the spiritual kingdom of God. Again, they chose king Saul by demanding that the physical kingdom be restored, which would rule from without, rejecting Jesus' spiritual teachings of a spiritual kingdom that would rule from within, ruled by David; by the spirit of Love. When tempted by the Pharisees as to which commandment was the greatest, Jesus said, *Love*.

Shortly after the reign of David, Israel and Judah are divided, illustrating a separation between the Mind and Heart, the kings of Israel and Judah symbolizing the spirits that rule our mind and heart. As wars with surrounding nations continue, the northern tribes of Israel are dispersed; leaving the southern tribe of Judah to enlarge, as seen in her first king, *Rehoboam,* meaning *a people has enlarged*. The tribe of Judah would end up being held captive by *the king of Babylon,* which translates to *the spirit of confusion*. Let's fast-forward down through history and see what led to the captivity and confusion of the Jews of Judea.

And the Jews' passover was at hand, and Jesus went up to Jerusalem, And found in the temple those that sold oxen and sheep and doves, and the changers of money sitting: And when he had made a scourge of small cords, he drove them out of the temple, and the sheep, and the oxen; and poured out the changers' money, and overthrew the tables; and said unto them that sold doves, Take these things hence; make not my Father's house an house of merchandise. John 2:13-16

The *tables* in the temple symbolize the *"fleshy tables of the heart"* (2 Corinthians 3:3), upon which we have sold a vast array of false images. We have become spiritual merchants, buying and selling in our *Father's house,* in the temple— in our heart. The Jews serve as our greatest teachers, illustrating man's custom of buying and selling spiritually by becoming merchants themselves. If we rewind the reel of Jewish history, we find that the Jews left the land of protection to become merchants. They traveled to Greece and Italy to buy and sell their wares. They settled as traders in Spain, France, and other parts of the Roman Empire, and later migrated to Germany, Poland and Russia, to name a few. They became prosperous in these countries they left God's protection for, a prosperity that fueled the flames of anger that would destroy them. Prosperity and wealth is not against God, it is part of God's abundance. But when it becomes a god, when we put it before the Almighty God, we break God's Commandment, and in doing so, separate ourselves from God's protection, which Jerusalem symbolizes. The Jews were told to remain in Jerusalem, but once again they disobey God's word.

No man can serve two masters: for either he will hate the one, and love the other; or else he will hold to the one, and despise the other. You cannot serve God and mammon. Matthew 6:24

It is written, *"For the love of money is the root of all evil."* Money gives us a sense of security, making us feel comfortable, giving us peace of mind by giving us some control over our life. It is not the money, which has the power to do a lot of good, that is evil, but the love of money; greed, the lustful emotion at the root of the negative and destructive energy in the world. This lust for money, which prevents one from seeking the source of their spiritual power, creates enmity between the two powers. Monetary power is a form of empowerment, but it is a spurious power, as is the peace that it brings, which will fail when the money fails (Genesis 47:15). It's the authentic spiritual power (not the false spiritual power generated through spiritual greed) that brings authentic peace to the heart, which will not fail us in troubling times. We empower the evil by preventing the inherent good that comes to us when we stop resisting the spiritual power of our heart. The word *mammon* means *confidence, i.e. wealth, personified.* The Jews had put their confidence in money, but no amount of money could save them in their time of trouble.

The Jew's Judgment for Disobedience

And that no man might buy or sell, save he that had the mark, or the name of the beast, or the number of his name. Revelation 13:17

By becoming merchants, we authorize our own destruction. No man can buy or sell without receiving the mark, which is to be marked for destruction, the physical revealing the spiritual.

Here is wisdom. Let him that hath understanding count the number of the beast: for it is the number of a man; and his number is six hundred three score and six. Revelation 13:18

Six hundred (600) three score (60) and (0) six (6). If you write this number out, you get *6006006.* Right to left, or left to right, it's the same number: six million, six thousand, and six, the number of Jews put to death in the Holocaust.

And there was given unto him a mouth speaking great things and blasphemies; and power was given unto him to continue forty and two months. Revelation 13:5

When we are disobedient, we raise up our own judge and judgment. The Jew's judge was Hitler, and their judgment was the Holocaust. Judgment comes to get us back on track, and in a place of protection, as was the case with the Jews who escaped the Holocaust, many of whom returned as Zionists to Jerusalem, the place of God's protection. The judge of the Jews was given *forty and two months* to execute his judgment. Forty two was also the year, according to several sources, that the Final Solution, the mass extermination of Jews in Europe, was ordered. Because God loves his children, He enacted the cosmic law of cause and effect. Disobedience brings forth judgment.

To reiterate, *Israel* symbolizes the *Mind,* which could not excel because of fear and lies. Israel was unable to perceive of the spiritual word or law of God, having eyes that could not see and ears that could not hear, uncircumcised in the spiritual sense of the word. After Israel, came Judah, who upon entering the land promised them, were circumcised for the second time, illustrating their ability to perceive, and conceive of the spiritual word of God. They went on to bring down the wall that separated them from the Promised Land, allowing them to see the enemies inhabiting the land. *Judah* symbolizes the *Heart,* the seven nations symbolizing the spiritual impurities dwelling in our heart, which keep us from taking possession of the joyful life promised us. In the beginning, Judah was obedient, fighting against these nations they were to drive out. But in time, they would disobey God's word by making marriages with these nations, illustrating their failure to drive these impurities out of the heart, not turning to God *with her whole heart.*

...Hast thou seen that which backsliding Israel hath done? she is gone upon every high mountain and under every green tree and there played the harlot. And I said after she had done all these things, Turn thou unto me. But she returned not. And her treacherous sister Judah saw it. And I saw, when for all the causes whereby backsliding Israel committed adultery I had put her away, and given her a bill of divorce; yet her

treacherous sister Judah feared not, but went and played the harlot also... And it came to pass through the lightness of her whoredom, that she defiled the land... And yet for all this her treacherous sister Judah hath not turned unto me with her whole heart, but feignedly, saith the Lord...The backsliding Israel hath justified herself more than treacherous Judah... Return thou backsliding Israel... and I will not cause mine anger to fall upon you... Only acknowledge thine iniquity... Turn, O backsliding children... and I will take you one of a city, and two of a family, and I will bring you to Zion. Jeremiah 3:6-14

Chapter Four
Israel of the Gentiles

We have seen the rebelliousness of Israel, and the disobedience of Judah. But the rejection of God's word would not be exclusive to the Jews. When the spiritual word of God returned two thousand years ago, it was rejected by *the People of Israel,* so His spiritual truth was given to a new people, the pagans, whose practices included the worshipping of molten images, likened to Israel's worshipping of the gold calf in the wilderness. These pagans were open-minded; open to the spiritual word of God, and came to be called *Gentiles.* But it would not be long before they too would reject it, returning to their worshipping of false images. They, along with the Jews, the People of Israel, came against the word of God, coming against spiritual truth.

The kings of the earth stood up, and the rulers assembled together, against the Lord, and against his anointed. For truly, in this city, both Herod, and Pontius Pilate, with the Gentiles and the People of Israel were gathered together against thy holy Servant Jesus, whom thou hast anointed.   Acts 4:26,27

These pagans worshipped the Great goddess Diana of the Ephesians, whom Demetrius, a silversmith made shrines of, the sale of which was now being threatened by this Jesus of Nazareth, whose teachings condemned the worshipping of images or *other gods,* citing God's Commandment.

Moreover ye see and hear, that not alone at Ephesus, but almost throughout all Asia, this Paul hath persuaded and turned away much people, saying that they be no gods, which are made with hands, So that not only this our craft is in danger to be set at nought; but also that the temple of the great goddess Diana should be despised, and her magnificence should be destroyed, whom all Asia and the world worshippeth. And when they had heard these sayings, they were full of wrath, and cried out, Great is Diana of the Ephesians. Acts 19:26-28

Paul, rooted in Jewish tradition, was a zealot when it came to the law. And the popularity of the spiritual teachings of another Jew named Jesus, would only serve to further Paul's cause following his conversion. It was to these spiritual teachings that the pagans were drawn. The pagan religion was predominant at the time, the great image of that day corresponding to the great religious image of today.

And the angel said unto me, Wherefore didst thou marvel? I will tell thee the mystery of the woman, and of the beast that carrieth her...
Revelation 17:7

The woman of two thousand years ago was the great goddess Diana, the beast that carried or supported her being the pagan religion. But spiritually, the *woman* symbolizes *flesh;* an invisible flesh that is one with the *beast*, symbolizing the *false image, belief* or *word*. As we continue our journey with Israel of the Gentiles, we will identify the woman and the beast in the most predominate and powerful religion in recorded history.

And the merchants of the earth shall weep and mourn over her; for no man buyeth their merchandise anymore. Revelation 18:11

The *merchants of the earth* are those that traffic in religious images or beliefs. But as the world moves away from religion and into spirituality, these merchants will be hard pressed to find anyone interested in buying their merchandise. What will put an end to the buying and selling of these false religious images, is spiritual truth. The word of truth, which came to earth through Jesus two thousand years ago, put an end to the buying and selling of images made by hand, literally, briefly. But today, in what is the spiritual era of Jacob, it will be the spiritual return of Jesus to the earth; the return of truth to the heart that will stop us from trafficking in these worthless false images or beliefs, which we bought into with our mind and sold to our heart.

Moreover, brethren, I would not that ye should be ignorant, how that all our fathers were under the cloud, and all passed through the sea... And did all eat the same spiritual meat; And did drink the same spiritual drink...1 Corinthians 10:1,3,4

Jesus is returning to the individual, with the spiritual meat of spiritual truth, which does not support the false religious image. In drinking of the spiritual drink, we pass over from thinking with a carnal mind to thinking with a spiritual mind. In eating of the spiritual meat, we pass over from our old way of believing to a new way of believing through obedience to the spiritual works of God's Word. These represent our two spiritual passovers, coinciding with our two spiritual circumcisions— of the mind and of the heart.

Those deeply rooted in the carnal-minded doctrines of religion will show contempt for the spiritual word of God, reflected in their anger, which destroyed the embodiment of spiritual truth two thousand years ago. Anger is born out of fear, and this unholy spirit of fear is what prevents one from letting go of these images or beliefs. But there will be more and more, who upon hearing spiritual truth, within or without, will stop buying the merchandise of the beastly religious image. It will be our love of truth, not our need to be right, that will end the reverence we show toward these erroneous beliefs, whose only power comes through the fear and lies they perpetuate. No longer placing value on this merchandise of false religious beliefs, the merchants within and without will be out of business, for good!

The Gentiles of two thousand years ago had left behind the graven images by hearing the word of God spoken through Jesus, as the children of Israel heard the voice of God through Samuel. But having a propensity for images, they would choose a king, as Israel chose Saul, who would form an image out of God's word through carnal interpretations, which this Gentile Israel believed, being led to believe in the Son, as opposed to obeying the spiritual works of the Father (John 10:32-38). With the return of spiritual truth comes an opportunity to stop worshipping the false religious beliefs of today. Diana's counterpart is called, *"Babylon the Great, the Mother of harlots and abominations of the earth,"* the Mother Church, the cause of so much confusion.

So he carried me away in the spirit into the wilderness: and I saw a woman sit upon a scarlet coloured beast, full of names of blasphemy, having seven heads and ten horns... And here is the mind which hath wisdom. The seven heads are seven mountains, on which the woman sitteth. And there are seven kings: five are fallen, and one is, and the other is not yet come; and when he cometh, he must continue a short space.   Revelation 17:3,9,10

The *seven heads* or *seven mountains* represent the seven hills upon which the city of Rome, home of the Vatican, is situated. The *seven kings* represent *seven popes,* all of whom shared the same name. Paul. An in-depth research done in the early sixties revealed that Pope Paul VI was so evil; they proclaimed they would never again name a pope by that name, so they prefixed it with John. Pope John Paul I, the seventh, *the other,* would *continue a short space,* being in power for only thirty-four days, fulfilling this prophecy in 1978. The *woman* today represents the Catholic Church, Israel of the Gentiles, Moab, the first fruit of Lot, born of incest, inbred thoughts, the beginning of iniquity for this Gentile Israel. And after Moab, was born Ammon, the second fruit of Lot, which was born when Martin Luther protested against certain catholic beliefs, for which he was excommunicated in 1521, giving birth to the Protestant Church and her many Trinity offshoots. It is upon the teachings of Paul that the Church was built!

Israel demands a King

...Give us a king to judge us. And Samuel prayed unto the Lord. And the Lord said unto Samuel, Hearken unto the voice of the people in all that they say unto thee: for they have not rejected thee, but they have rejected me, that I should not reign over them. According to all the works which they have done since the day that I brought them up out of Egypt even unto this day, wherewith they have forsaken me, and served other gods, so do they also unto thee. Now therefore hearken unto their voice: howbeit yet protest solemnly unto them and shew them the manner of the king that shall reign over them. And Samuel told all the words of the Lord unto the people that asked him a king. And he said, This will be the manner of the king that shall reign over you: He will take your sons, and appoint them for himself, for his chariots, and to be his horsemen; and some shall run before his chariots. And he will appoint him captains over thousands, and captains over fifties; and will set them to ear the ground, and to reap his harvest, and to make his instruments of war, and instruments of his chariots. And he will take your daughters to be confectionaries, and to be cooks, and to be bakers. And he will take your fields, and your vineyards, and your oliveyards, even the best of them, and give them to his servants. And he will take your menservants, and your maidservants, and your goodliest men, and your asses, and put them to his work. He will take the tenth of your sheep: and ye shall be his servants. And ye shall cry out in that day because of your king which ye have chosen you; and the Lord will not hear you in that day. Nevertheless the people refused to obey the voice of Samuel; and

they said, Nay; but we will have a king over us; That we may be like all the nations; and that our king may judge us, and go out before us, and fight our battles. 1 Samuel 8:6-20

If you take these words and convert them into modern day terms, you can easily make the connection to the church, and how it operates. For example, the *sheep* symbolize the *flock* or *congregation.* To *take the tenth* of the sheep is requiring them to pay *ten percent* of their income to the Church. What I have found to be so prevalent in writing this book is that when given a choice to serve God and be free, or serve man-made images and be in bondage, man choice bondage. The only reason that makes any sense is that we laid the foundation for this propensity long ago when we chose lies over truth. Lies lead us into bondage, while the truth makes us free. We have become so accustomed to being in bondage, having limiting ideologies ruling us, freedom feels foreign to us, it makes us uncomfortable, and so it continues to elude us. Take Adam and Eve for example, who chose to accept a belief that opposed God's word, losing the freedom of the garden. Or the children of Israel, who chose the bondage of Egypt over the freedom of the Promised Land, living and dying under another type of bondage, under the limitations of the carnal law, never tasting of the freedom that comes from obeying the spiritual law of God. And their children, who tasted of that freedom in the Promised Land, yet chose to forfeit that freedom by disobeying God's word, making marriages with the nations they were to drive out.

Israel wanted a king to judge them, and fight their battles for them, just as people want their religious leaders to decide what is right and wrong, so they don't have to battle with these decisions themselves. We have long since forgotten how to trust in, and take direction from, our internal anointing, which guides us into the light of truth through the power of our holy spirit. We prefer to have the unholy spirit of fear rule our mind and tell us lies, then to allow the holy spirit of our heart to bring us the truth that will result in a spiritual and physical freedom that seems to petrify us.

Saul was the king that ruled over Israel of Judaism, but he also represents a spirit that rules over Israel of the Gentiles. With a new Israel, came a new Saul. The name has changed, but the spirit is one and the same. Paul, referred to as Apostle to the Gentiles, was not chosen to be among the twelve so that we may see that there are two foundations that have been laid. One foundation has twelve pillars, represented by the twelve apostles, the foundation upon which the holy city of Jerusalem is built. The other foundation has one pillar, represented by the one apostle, Paul, upon which the city of Babylon is built. Paul laid his foundation through the words he spoke, mixing carnal law with spiritual truth; mixing milk with meat, which is unlawful. It is the cause of all the confusion and dissension among Christians today. The word *Babylon* means *confusion*.

And I brethren, could not speak unto you as spiritual, but as unto carnal, even as unto babes in Christ. I have fed you with milk, and not with meat: for hitherto ye were not able to bear it, neither yet now are ye able. For ye are yet carnal: for whereas there is among you envying, and strife, and divisions, are ye not yet carnal, and walk as men?
I Corinthians 3:1-3

Paul did speak to them with regard to the *carnal* and the *spiritual*, mixing the two, failing to allegorize. It would have been far better had he chosen one or the other. A zealot for the law, he became a hindrance to those tending toward the spirit, often finding fault with the Apostles of spiritual truth. He was a chosen vessel, chosen to show the detrimental effect of mixing carnal and spiritual, which goes beyond the physical slaughter of the disciples of the Lord, and into the spiritual slaughter that takes place because of the confusion caused by his doctrine. *Paul*, solely responsible for the doctrines of the churches in Asia, and their rules and regulations, symbolizes *organized religion*. John, of the twelve, instructs us through the second and third chapters of Revelation, to overcome the lies that exist in the doctrines of organized religion. The word *Paul* means *to come to an end*. It is the false doctrines of religion that are to come to an end.

We learn from the Dead Sea Scrolls that Paul was a liar, which is how both Jews, who kept the carnal law, and spiritual Christians, who obeyed the spiritual works, would have viewed him. It was his doctrine that is responsible for the carnal interpretations that have been assigned to God's Word over the years. Paul laid the foundation upon which Christianity was built, his teachings the source of the confusion. But on the more important spiritual level, Paul represents the liar within us, which has sold us on false beliefs, which are *to come to an end* within us.

Israel of Judaism chose Saul because they wanted someone to judge them and fight their battles for them. Israel of the Gentiles chose Paul for the same reason. Most Christian doctrines lean solely on the teachings of Paul, the religious institutions operating through a set of by-laws, which the people willingly choose to obey. They pay their tithes, hiring someone to tell them what to believe, a belief that keeps them from fighting the ongoing internal battle between their own mind and heart, which can only be won through an internal anointing, through which they would gain the spiritual strength they need to be delivered, made free of their spiritual and physical bondages.

But the anointing which ye have received of him abideth in you, and ye need not that any man teach you: but as the same anointing teacheth you of all things, and is truth, and is no lie, and even as it hath taught you, ye shall abide in him. I John 2:27

Howbeit when he, the Spirit of truth, is come, he will guide you into all truth... John 16:13

If we would trust God by having confidence in our internal guidance system, we would have no need for these erroneous religious beliefs, or the self-appointed prophets and priests that push or traffic them.

The prophets prophesy falsely, and the priests bear rule by their means; and my people love to have it so: and what will ye do in the end thereof?
Jeremiah 5:31

But many are still allowing someone, or something, to do their thinking for them, and then they judge themselves according to that wrong way of thinking, leaving the righteous judgment undone. If they would shut out the incessant fear and noise that governs their mind through these man-made dogmas, they would activate the holy spirit of their heart, which would bring them into the truth of what they need to judge in themselves. Once they begin to connect with truth, as Peter, a piece of rock, connected with Jesus, they can lay a sure foundation through sound doctrine, as opposed to laying a foundation of sand though an unsound doctrine. They will enter a spiritual church, where they will worship the Father *in spirit and in truth*.

Jesus saith unto her, Woman, believe me, the hour cometh, when ye shall neither in this mountain, nor yet at Jerusalem, worship the Father. Ye worship ye know not what: we know what we worship: for salvation is of the Jews. But the hour cometh, and now is, when the true worshippers shall worship the Father in spirit and in truth: for the Father seeketh such to worship him. God is a Spirit: and they that worship him must worship him in spirit and in truth. John 4:21-24

Jesus said, *salvation is of the Jews,* reason enough to question Paul's teachings on salvation seeing as he was chosen Apostle to the Gentiles, not the Jews.

Through God's spiritual judgment, symbolized by the twelve apostles or twelve sons of Jacob, we rend our spiritual kingdoms of mind and heart out from the rule of Saul, and hand it over to David. No longer ruling ourselves by this demanding, oppressive, tyrannical regime, which we put into power by allowing fear and lies to rule our mind, we will govern ourselves in the spirit of love and with the word of truth, made free through the purification of our heart.

And Samuel said unto Saul, I will not return with thee: for thou hast rejected the word of the Lord, and the Lord hath rejected thee from being king over Israel... And Samuel said unto him, The Lord hath rent the kingdom of Israel from thee this day, and hath given it to a neighbor of thine, that is better than thou. 1 Samuel 15:26,28

The word *Samuel* means *heard of God*. When we listen to the voice of God, which speaks to us through the spirit of our heart when we silence the external voices and noise of our mind, we will reject the spirit that rules us from our head. A spirit that demands we adhere to self-imposed laws, which have no power to transform our heart, causing us to remain in bondage. We will set up something better, a spirit that rules us from our heart, having the power to make us free. *King David* symbolizes *A Spirit* that persuades us *to love* ourselves. *King Saul* symbolizes *A Spirit* that *demands* we rule ourselves through fear. The kingdom of Saul was given to David two thousand years ago at the coming of Jesus; at which time we were to no longer to look to a physical kingdom without, but to a spiritual kingdom within.

...The kingdom of God cometh not with observation: Neither shall they say, Lo here! or, lo there! for, behold, the kingdom of God is within you.
Luke 17:20,21

But the Jews, the People of Israel, demanded a physical king and kingdom, as their ancestors demanded Saul, rejecting the idea of a spiritual king and kingdom. And their counterpart, Israel of the Gentiles, followed suit, assigning carnal interpretations to God's spiritual word, looking to a physical kingdom ruled by a physical king named Jesus. The Messianic reign, a parallel to the reign of David, preached a spiritual kingdom, which is why David was not permitted to build a physical temple. That was done by Solomon in the following reign, representing the reign of pseudo-Christianity that followed the Messianic reign, the physical house of the Lord that Solomon built representing the church, which Paul built up through his own doctrine.

But king Solomon loved many strange women, together with the daughter of Pharaoh, women of the Moabites, Ammonites, Edomites, Zidonians, and Hittites; Of the nations concerning which the Lord said unto the children of Israel, Ye shall not go in to them, neither shall they come in unto you: for surely they will turn away your heart after their gods: Solomon clave unto these in love. And he had seven hundred wives, princesses, and three hundred concubines: and his wives turned away his heart...his heart was not perfect with the Lord his God, as was the heart of David his father. 1 Kings 11:1-4

David was thirty years old when he began to reign, and he reigned forty years. In Hebron he reigned over Judah seven years and six months: and in Jerusalem he reigned thirty and three years over all Israel and Judah.
2 Samuel 5:4,5

Jesus, like David, was *thirty* years of age when he was given authority, teaching the spiritual kingdom of God, which he did until the death of his physical body at age *thirty and three*. This concept of a spiritual kingdom lived until it was destroyed by the carnal mind; by the literal interpretations of the man-made doctrines of the Christian religion.

Is not this David, of whom they sang one to another in dances, saying, Saul slew his thousands, and David his ten thousands. 1 Samuel 29:5

Note: *thousands* and *ten thousands;* a factor of 10 to 1, which when applied to the number of years in the Bible, provides important information as to our own timeline.

David ruled *Israel* and *Judah* for 40 years and 6 months, as the spiritual doctrine of Jesus ruled the *Mind* and *Heart* of Christians for 460 years, applying the 10 to 1 factor. By 460AD, teachings of a spiritual kingdom gave way to teachings of a physical kingdom called heaven, taking the focus off of the internal and putting it on the external, this religious iniquity increasing over the next 1500 years, until 1960, when the foundation for spiritual truth was re-established through a revelation that exposed this religious iniquity. A second revelation further spiritualized the teachings of the first, giving us insight into the two spiritual kingdoms. It took 46 years to build the temple. 1960 + 46 = 2006, a year discovered in the mathematical code of the Bible, which, not surprisingly, has to do with the spiritual sacrifice that is to take place in the spiritual temple.

Destroy this temple, and in three days I will raise it up. Then said the Jews, Forty and six years was this temple in building... John 2:19,20

The Jews did not understand what Jesus meant when he said he could raise the temple in three days because they could not think spiritually, never drinking of the spiritual drink. Not only was Jesus referring to his body, but to the spiritual temple that is to be raised on the third day, which the world entered with the new millennium; the beginning of the third-thousandth year since the physical temple of Jesus was destroyed, and in which the spiritual temple is to be restored

The reign of David ended when he was 70, which ties in with the destruction of the physical temple in Jerusalem in 70AD. The spiritual temple is the heart, and what is to reside in the heart is truth. But when that truth is crucified, the spiritual temple is left in ruins. The reign of Solomon, pseudo-Christianity, began around 400AD, the minds and hearts of Christians no longer ruled by spiritual truth, but by religious iniquity. Solomon loved *"many strange women,"* the *women* symbolizing *flesh,* layer upon layer upon layer of flesh formed by the many strange doctrines of Christianity, forming the carnal mind, which prevents a spiritual understanding of God's Word. Solomon's reign led to a division in the kingdoms, between *Israel* and *Judah,* illustrating a division in our spiritual kingdoms, between our *Mind* and *Heart.* Israel was ruled by king Jeroboam and Judah was ruled by king Rehoboam. *Jeroboam* means *the people will contend,* the word *contend* meaning *to strive (as at battle), or in controversy or debate; to dispute,* revealing the contentious spirit ruling the mind. This is where our mind begins to come against the truth, resisting the holy spirit that brings that truth.

As Pharaoh drew near, the Children of Israel lifted up their eyes: Here, Egypt marching after them! They were exceedingly afraid. And the Children of Israel cried out to YHWH, they said to Moshe: Is it because there were no graves in Egypt that you have taken us out to die in the wilderness? What is it that you have done to us, bringing us out of Egypt? Is this not the very word that we spoke to you in Egypt, saying: Let us alone, that we may serve Egypt. Indeed, better for us serving Egypt than our dying in the wilderness! Exodus 14:10-12
(The Five Books of Moses)

This dispute took place as they were passing over, as they were leaving behind the old land of bondage to enter the new land of freedom. As soon as we make a decision to change our life for the better, we can count on fear and doubt getting in the way, feeding us lies, causing us to resist the holy spirit that makes this transition possible. Israel contended with Moses at their baptism in the Red Sea, as the Israel of the Gentiles contended with God's Word when it came to water baptism.

Go ye therefore, and teach all nations, baptizing them in the name of the Father, and of the Son, and of the Holy Spirit. Matthew 28:19

Here we have an error in translation. The disciples were to teach baptism *in the name of the Father*, baptism *of the Son*, and baptism *of the Holy Spirit*. Baptism *in the name of the Father* is a *physical* baptism in the literal name of Jesus, the son carrying on the name of his father, as it is written, *"I am come in my Father's name."* Baptism *of the Son* is a spiritual baptism, into the spiritual name, being immersed in truth from within, which no man has the power to do. Baptism *of the Holy Spirit*, as with truth, takes place within. No man has the power to perform these two spiritual baptisms. John the Baptist baptized the people with water in the Jordan, yet he pointed to one that would come after him, and baptize them with fire and the holy spirit. Clearly, these are spiritual baptisms, because Jesus baptized no one.

When therefore the Lord knew how the Pharisees had heard that Jesus made and baptized more disciples than John, (though Jesus himself baptized not, but his disciples,)... John 4:1,2

It was the disciples who baptized the people, and only in the name, one assigned to the Father for a period of two thousand years, in the carnal era of Isaac, which ended with the new millennium. Physical baptism is over!

Then Peter said unto them, Repent, and be baptized every one of you in the name of Jesus Christ, for the remission of sins, and ye shall receive the gift of the Holy Spirit. Acts 2:38

And he commanded them to be baptized in the name of the Lord...
Acts 10:48

Our first baptism, in this new spiritual era, is unto repentance, which takes place in a spiritual Jordan when we humble ourselves by admitting that the place we are at in our life is not where we want to be. The word *repent* means *to think differently, i.e. reconsider, or morally to feel compunction.* Compunction is a strong uneasiness caused by a sense of remorse or regret, which occurs when we begin to feel uncomfortable with our beliefs, or with the way our life is going. When we begin to regret the decisions we have made based on those beliefs, or begin to feel a sense of remorse for what we have done, not only to ourselves, but to others. It is in this humbled state that we enter a symbolic Jordan, becoming a spiritual Gentile, having an open mind, willing to be taught a new and better way. This baptism unto repentance is where we first begin to feel the effects of our holy spirit. We feel it first at the mind level as it begins to influence the thoughts of our mind, giving us the strength to begin the process of changing our life. With a willingness to change our life, to be drawn out of the restrictions imposed by our wrong way of thinking, our spiritual baptism of the son begins. The power of this truth holds back the fear and lies of our mind so we can make the transition, illustrated at the Red Sea, and again at the Jordan River, where the waters were held back long enough for them to cross over and begin their spiritual works. Baptism symbolizes the process of being made spiritually pure by being drawn out of the water, symbolizing the waste in our life. *"She named him Moses, and said, Because I drew him out of the water.* Exodus 2:10

Then cometh Jesus from Galilee to Jordan to John, to be baptized of him. But John forbad him, saying, I have need to be baptized of thee, and comest thou to me? And Jesus answering said unto him, Suffer it to be so now: for thus it becometh us to fulfil all righteousness…
Matthew 3:13-15

John baptized Jesus to illustrate that it is our holy spirit that draws us out of our old way of life, the *spirit* symbolized by the *dove* that descended upon Jesus at his baptism. But it will be the culmination of the spirit and the word, through spiritual works, that will make us free of our unsatisfactory, unprofitable, or burdensome way of life. Overcoming what formed this life we no longer take much joy in, completes our spiritual baptism of the son and of the holy spirit.

John answered, saying unto them all, I indeed baptize you with water; but one mightier than I cometh, the latchet of whose shoes I am not worthy to unloose: he shall baptize you with the Holy Spirit and with fire: Whose fan is in his hand, and he will thoroughly purge his floor, and will gather the wheat into his garner; but the chaff he will burn with fire unquenchable.   Luke 3:16,17

The *fan,* also symbolizing the *spirit,* does the separating. Like the wind, it fans the flame that consumes our iniquity by bringing us truth. Our baptism with *fire* takes place as we *judge* the beliefs below our thoughts, separating the chaff from the wheat, the lies from the truth, the lies consumed through the works of this spiritual judgment.

And when the day of Pentecost was fully come, they were all with one accord in one place. And suddenly there came a sound from heaven as of a rushing mighty wind, and it filled all the house where they were sitting. And there appeared unto them cloven tongues like as of fire, and it sat upon each of them. And they were all filled with the Holy Spirit, and began to speak with other tongues, as the Spirit gave them utterance.
Acts 2:1-4

There are seven weeks between Passover and the day of Pentecost. The word *seven* means *to seven times oneself.* Seven pertains to the spiritual, and is associated with the spiritual process, which takes place between the time we decide to pass over from our old life and the time when that which prevents us from having a new life, is consumed, which is our spiritual day of Pentecost. The *fire,* symbolizing *judgment,* consumes the unholy spirit of our mind and the unrighteous word of our heart, creating the void that gives birth to a new creation; a new heaven and earth; a new mind and heart. Likened unto *cloven tongues,* this spiritual fire separates what is holy and true from what is not, leaving us speaking a new language, the language of truth, which results in a new life (Revelation 21:1-5).

All that took place physically in the era of Isaac (baptism, anointing, fasting, healing, speaking in tongues, casting out devils, etc.) are now, in the final era of Jacob or era of Spirit, to take place spiritually. Any physical demonstrations of these are associated with the negative aspect of the era of *Isaac,* which is *mockery*. Physical baptism in the name of the Father, Son, and Holy Spirit has no legitimacy. It is based on a lie because no man has the power or authority to baptize us of the son or of the Holy Spirit. Baptism of the son is to be immersed in truth. Baptism of the Holy Spirit is to be immersed in Love. It is through spiritual baptism of the son that we are clothed in white raiment, adorned in a spiritual wedding garment, becoming a spiritual bride, receiving a new name, the spiritual name of truth. Our baptism of the Holy Spirit is complete when we are totally immersed in our holy spirit, which takes place when love dominates fear, as it is written, *"perfect love casteth out fear"* (I John 4:18).

When the word of truth dominates the heart, so too does the spirit of love, the good spirit and word driving the evil spirits and word out of the heart. This purified state makes us a spiritual virgin, and as it is written, *"a virgin shall conceive and bear a son"* (Isaiah 7:14), the son symbolizing the complete development or maturation of the soul through the highest degree of conception of truth in that spiritual womb called the heart. The holy spirit is the divine power or spiritual energy that delivers the gift, which is the seed or word of God; truth. We complete the revitalization or quickening of our holy spirit through truth, so you can see why this erroneous belief in a physical baptism based on a lie is so detrimental to the soul. It started with the Catholic Church, *"Babylon the Great, the Mother of harlots;"* the false trinity doctrines born of the Catholic Church. They make up Israel of the Gentiles, and as their counterpart, Israel of Judaism, they failed because of the iniquity of their mind, *Israel* symbolizing our *Mind.*

Chapter Five
Judah of the Gentiles

Israel and Judah, two groups of people, represented among the Jewish and Gentile nations. Israel of the Gentiles refers to two of these religious factions, Catholic and Trinity. Now we will identify the religious group that falls under the category of Judah of the Gentiles. Judah was the tribe separated out for David's sake, for the sake of the spiritual kingdom of God. Israel symbolizes the Mind, which ruled by the unholy spirit of fear has caused her to buy into lies, while *Judah* symbolizes the *Heart*. What comes out of Judah reveals what proceeds out of the heart, be it holy or unholy, good or evil. John and Jesus, embodying the Spirit and Word of God, came out of the tribe of Judah, revealing the positive attributes of the Heart; love and truth. The beheading of John the Baptist and crucifixion of Jesus the Christ illustrate what has taken place in the heart of man, the holy spirit of love and word of truth usurped by the unholy spirit of fear and word of lies. Spirit and Word, the two witnesses of the heart, appearing in physical form two thousand years ago in the era of *Isaac;* in the era of *mockery*.

And when they had platted a crown of thorns, they put it upon his head, and a reed in his right hand: and they bowed the knee before him, and mocked him, saying, Hail, King of the Jews! Matthew 27:29

Israel is also associated with the thoughts of the mind, and Judah with the actions of the heart. Mockery, defined as a specific action of ridicule or derision, takes place in the heart, against the righteous truth of the heart. When a thought of the mind is accepted as truth by the heart through the power of emotion, that thought becomes a sown seed or spoken word. The mouth of the mind will then speak what the heart believes to be true, as it is written, *"for of the abundance of the heart, the mouth speaketh"* (Luke 6:45). Like a seed that is sown in the earth, a word or belief, true or false, grows, and in the process of time brings forth, manifesting in our life through our experiences, be they positive or negative, constructive or destructive, desirable or undesirable, as every seed is after its own kind; good or evil. Judah was separated out for Jerusalem's sake, for the mother's sake. *"Jerusalem… the mother of us all"* (Galatians 4:26). Judah was called out of all the tribes to bring the name to Jerusalem, as the mother needs the name so that her son is not born a *bastard*.

A bastard shall not enter into the congregation of the Lord; even to his tenth generation shall he not enter into the congregation of the Lord.
Deuteronomy 23:2

You will often find *Judah* and *Jerusalem* in connection with one another because they represent the *name* and the *mother* who bears the name. The Father's physical name was announced in the physical era of Isaac.

…but in Isaac shall thy seed be called.   Romans 9:7

The word *called* means *to bid, call forth, whose surname was called*. God called a man forth from the tribe of Judah to announce His name to the world, the name of the Father carried down through the son, as Jesus said, *"I am come in my Father's name."* The word *seed* means *something sown;* from the root word meaning *to draw out*. Jesus, called the Son of God, was the manifestation of the seed or word of God, who came to draw out the Jews of Judea, Judah, and bring them into the name of the Father through physical baptism, as had been done, in type, with their ancestors fifteen hundred years earlier, in the

Red Sea. But they rejected Jesus as Messiah, rejecting God's holy name, rejecting His spiritual word or holy seed, that once conceived of in the heart brings salvation to the soul, healing the soul.

Israel of the Gentiles rejected the name when they accepted a baptism based on a lie, but out of this Gentile Israel God called forth a new people that would restore baptism in the name of Jesus. This people, who received the name through water baptism, were called Pentecostals, and their church, once organized, was called The United Pentecostal Church or UPC. This is Judah of the Gentiles. God has been called by many names throughout the ages, such as El-Shaddai, Yahweh, and Yehovah. And it was the tribe of Judah that was called out to bear the name. God's new name was announced to the world in the beginning of the era associated with Judah, in the era of Isaac; an era that marked the beginning of water baptism in the name of Jesus or Jehoshua. But knowledge of this true baptism would be confined to the grave four hundred years after its inception, where it remained for fifteen hundred years, the same number of years that transpired between Israel's type and shadow baptism in the Red Sea thirty-five hundred years ago, and what was to be the reality of Judean Jews baptism in the Jordan River two thousand years ago.

As we leave the physical era of Isaac, and enter the spiritual era of Jacob, which coincides with the new millennium, we leave behind physical baptism. Baptism is now to take place spiritually in a symbolic Jordan. We get down to this Jordan by humbling ourselves to the new spiritual era. By letting go of the literal and taking hold of the spiritual. The word *Jordan* means *to descend, to go downwards, or conventionally to a lower region,* which the tribe of Judah illustrated by separating from the tribes of Israel, becoming the kingdom of the south, situated geographically downward, in a lower region, from Israel. Judah of the Gentiles,

Pentecostals, separated themselves from Israel of the Gentiles when it came to baptism. By humbling themselves to the true water baptism, this Gentile Judah symbolically entered the Jordan, being physically baptized into the physical name in the physical era of Isaac. Judah of the Gentiles brought the name up to Jerusalem symbolically through baptism in the name of Jesus.

Seventy weeks are determined upon thy people and upon thy holy city, to finish the transgression, and to make an end of sins, and to make reconciliation for iniquity, and to bring in everlasting righteousness, and to seal up the vision and prophecy, and to anoint the most Holy.
Daniel 9:24

The reign of Judah, Pentecostals, began in 1905 and ended in 1975, *seventy* years, tying in with the *seventy weeks*. They, as the Jews of Judea, were given seventy years to bring in righteousness through the assimilation of truth, finishing their transgression and ending their sin or iniquity. Jews and Christians have both failed to obey the spiritual word of God. The veil of religious iniquity remains, holding up God's holy seed, and polluting His holy name. The Jews failure to assimilate spiritual truth through spiritual obedience to God's spiritual law was manifested in the destruction of the temple in Jerusalem in 70AD.

The downfall of Judah of the Gentiles was their impatience. The same was true of Israel, who being referred to as Judah after passing through the Red Sea, became impatient while waiting for Moses to come down off the mount. It was in this impatience that they built an image, and worshipped it. The impatience associated with Judah can be found in the thirty-eighth chapter of Genesis, a story that breaks in on the Joseph story, seemingly out of place. But with a little understanding, we will find that it is precise in its insertion.

And it came to pass at that time, that Judah went down from his brethren, and turned in to a certain Adullamite, whose name was Hirah. Genesis 38:1

Judah went down from his brethren when the tribe of Judah separated from the tribes of Israel. The root meaning of the word *Hirah* is *to blanch (as with shame), but in the sense of splendor.* When we become aware that the beliefs we accepted as truth, were lies, we come into our own shame. But it is also in this shame that we have an opportunity to find splendor through the great white light of truth. *Judah went down from his brethren* when Judah of the Gentiles, upon receiving the truth pertaining to water baptism, separated themselves from their Trinity brothers. They entered a symbolic Jordan through their baptism, receiving the name, and entered a symbolic land of Canaan, bringing down the *wall of Jericho,* symbolizing the *wall of iniquity,* which began with Israel of the Gentiles' iniquity regarding water baptism.

And Judah saw there a daughter of a certain Canaanite, whose name was Shuah; and he took her and went in unto her. Genesis 38:2

The word *daughter* means *to build, begin to build, obtain children,* the feminine equivalent of the Hebrew word *ben,* meaning *son (as a builder of the family name).* The word *Shuah* goes to the root word meaning *to be free,* as we are made free through the spiritual family name; truth. Judah of the Gentiles received the name through their *"in the name of Jesus"* water baptism, the foundation upon which they were to build more truth. But like their counterpart, who became impatient, building a beastly image at Mount Sinai, they too became impatient, building a beastly spiritual image through a false belief, an imitation or mockery of truth. Judah is more than a tribe, more than a group of people. Judah is associated with the era of Isaac, which began two thousand years ago. The word

Isaac means *mockery;* a spirit that manifested itself in a physical mockery of God's Son, a show of contempt for God's holy seed made flesh. Judah brought forth three sons: Er, Onan, and Shelah, as the era of Isaac brought forth Israel, Judah, and Zion, all of which mocked the spiritual word of God.

And Er, Judah's firstborn, was wicked in the sight of the Lord; and the Lord slew him. And Judah said unto Onan, Go in unto thy brother's wife, and marry her, and raise up seed to thy brother. Genesis 38:7,8

Er represents *Israel,* Catholic and her Trinity children, the first born in the era of Isaac or period of mockery. They contended with God's Word when it came to water baptism, as Israel contended with God's servant, Moses at their baptism in the Red Sea. *Onan* represents *Judah,* Pentecost, the second born in the era of mockery. The seed or word that Pentecost was to raise up to Trinity, was the truth regarding water baptism, removing the iniquity of Israel, removing the illegitimate *"Father, Son, Holy Spirit"* baptism of Catholic and Trinity. But they would keep the glory for themselves, the holy seed or word of truth on the matter, wasted.

And Onan knew that the seed should not be his; and it came to pass, when he went in unto his brother's wife, that he spilled it on the ground, lest that he should give seed to his brother. Genesis 38:9

The reign of Israel of the Gentiles began around 400AD, the doctrine of which ruled the minds of Christians for approximately 1500 years, until the reign of Judah of the Gentiles in 1905. The truth revealed to Pentecost regarding water baptism should have been seed for Catholic and Trinity, removing the *iniquity of the house of Israel.*

Lie also upon thy left side, and lay the iniquity of the house of Israel upon it: according to the number of days that thou shalt lie upon it thou shalt bear the iniquity, according to the number of days, three hundred and ninety days: so shall thou bear the iniquity of the house of Israel. And when thou hast accomplished them, lie again on thy right side, and thou shalt bear the iniquity of the house of Judah forty days: I have appointed thee each day for a year... Ezekiel 4:4-6

Israel spent *three hundred and ninety* years in bondage in Egypt. Judah spent *forty* years in bondage in the wilderness, representing the bondage of our Mind and Heart. Er was slain, as was Israel, who died in the wilderness, in bondage to the iniquity of their mind. It would be their descendants that would bring down the *wall of Jericho,* symbolizing the *wall of iniquity* that was Israel's sin. Judah and Israel; Pentecost and Trinity, should have become one, just as our Heart and Mind is to become one. But in time, Pentecost would only add to the iniquity and divisions in Christianity.

The iniquity that caused Judah of the Gentiles to mock God's Word had to do with the promise of what they would receive following their baptism, this Pentecostal iniquity spreading like a fire gone out of control. When the iniquity of the mind is not overcome through the conception of truth in the heart, it forms into a false belief. Judah of the Gentiles took the iniquity to the next level, from a thought of the mind to a belief of the heart. Judah failed to drive the inhabitants out of the Promised Land, as Judah of the Gentiles failed to drive the unholy spirits and false beliefs out of that spiritual promised land called the heart.

As for the Jebusites the inhabitants of Jerusalem, the children of Judah could not drive them out: but the Jebusites dwell with the children of Judah unto this day. Joshua 15:63

And if it seem evil unto you to serve the Lord, choose you this day whom ye will serve; whether the gods which your fathers served that were on the other side of the flood, or the gods of the Amorites, in whose land ye dwell: but as for me and my house, we will serve the Lord.

Joshua 24:15

The *Jebusite* is the spirit to tread God's word of truth under foot, the *Amorite* is the spirit to declare what you believe as right, and what others believe as wrong, both of which apply to this Judah of the Gentiles. In addition to these, is the Perizzite, the spirit of isolation or separation. Pentecost isolated themselves from Trinity instead of communing with them, as the Heart needs to commune with the Mind. They could have learned from one another, taking out what was good in each, and moving on as one. But Judah of the Gentiles would conjure up even more lies out of impatience, adding to the veil or wall of iniquity, separating them from the truth. Following the death of Er and Onan, Tamar, Judah's daughter-in-law, is instructed to wait until the third son, Shelah, is grown. But she gets impatient waiting for what she was promised, and plays the harlot, committing adultery.

The Lord said also unto me in the days of Josiah the king, Hast thou seen that which backsliding Israel hath done? She is gone up upon every high tree, and there hath played the harlot. And I said after she had done all these things, Turn thou unto me. But she returned not. And her treacherous sister Judah saw it. And I saw, when for all the causes whereby backsliding Israel committed adultery I had put her away, and given her a bill of divorce; yet her treacherous sister Judah feared not, but went and played the harlot also. Jeremiah 3:6-8

The story of Judah and Tamar oddly interrupts the Joseph story to illustrate what has taken place in religion, and in us.

The word *Tamar* means *to be erect, a palm tree.* Judah of the Gentiles stood erect as a result of the truth they received on water baptism. But they got impatient for what they were promised after being baptized, which was the gift of the holy spirit. But instead of waiting for truth, they listened to their iniquity. How many times have we gotten impatient and listened to lies, instead of waiting for truth, as Tamar was to wait for Shelah.

And it came to pass, when she travailed, that the one put out his hand: and the midwife took and bound upon his hand a scarlet thread, saying, This came out first. And it came to pass, as he drew back his hand, that, behold, his brother came out: and she said, How hast thou broken forth: this breach be upon thee: therefore his name was called Pharez. Genesis 38:28,29

The word *Pharez* means *breach*; a breaking away from truth, the route this Gentile Judah would take, as we see in the generations in the book of Matthew (1:3), which leads to *Babylon* (1:11), meaning *confusion*. It is in our time of confusion that we cry out to God for clarity, as *Salathiel*, meaning *I have asked God*, is born after entering Babylon (1:12).

And afterward came out his brother, that had the scarlet thread upon his hand: and his name was called Zarah. Genesis 38:30

The word *Zarah* means *a rising of light*, symbolizing the resurrection of truth that is to take place in that spiritual earth called the heart. Tamar was to wait for Shelah, which is to wait for truth, the word *Shelah* meaning *to request or inquire*. Asking for truth as we go forward on our spiritual journey is a good thing, but we must not get impatient, or we will find ourselves right back where we started, which Jonathan, David's friend, illustrated for us by returning to the bloody house of Saul (2 Samuel 21:1). The word *Shelah* goes back to the same root as *Saul*, meaning *to demand*, revealing the unholy spirit behind the request or inquiry. And that is exactly what this Judah of the Gentiles would do. Driven by lust and impatience, they demanded what they believed was the promise, what they believed they were to receive following their baptism. Problem is, what they believed was a lie.

Then Peter said unto them, Repent, and be baptized every one of you in the name of Jesus Christ for the remission of sins, and ye shall receive the gift of the Holy Spirit. Acts 2:38

The promise was not the Holy Spirit. The promise was the gift of the Holy Spirit, what the Holy Spirit delivers, which is truth.

Now will I sing to my well-beloved touching his vineyard. My beloved hath a vineyard in a very fruitful hill: And he fenced it, and gathered out the stones thereof, and planted it with the choicest vine, and built a tower in the midst of it, and also made a winepress therein: and he looked that it should bring forth grapes, and it brought forth wild grapes. And now, O inhabitants of Jerusalem, and men of Judah, judge, I pray you, between me and my vineyard. What could have I done more to my vineyard, that I have not done in it?... And now go to; I will tell you what I will do to my vineyard : I will take away the hedge thereof, and it shall be eaten up; and break down the wall thereof, and it shall be trodden down: And I will lay it waste: it shall not be pruned, nor digged; but there shall come up briers and thorns: I will also command the clouds that they rain no rain upon it. Isaiah 5:1-6

The *vineyard* produces the fruit from which wine, symbolizing spirit, is made. Judah of the Gentiles was given every opportunity to bring forth good fruit. The *wild grapes* symbolize the *poisonous doctrines* of the Pentecostal Church. The *rain* symbolizes the *outpouring of God's spirit,* which they caused to be cut off because of the false belief they held pertaining to the Holy Spirit, one that drove Pentecostals, with great lust, to get the Holy Spirit or Holy Ghost.

My Holy Ghost Experience

In the mid-seventies, I visited a Pentecostal Church, where I witnessed this *"getting the Holy Ghost."* A seemingly somewhat reluctant woman was strongly encouraged to come up to the front of the church by several women. As the music played a rhythmic beat, they stood around her chanting something that sounded like *"jeda, jeda, jeda."* She began to imitate the sound, first slowly and then faster and faster and faster, until she began to talk in what sounded to me like a bunch of gibberish, which they interpreted as speaking in tongues. This caused great excitement in the women, who said, over and over again, *"She's got the Holy Ghost."*

Pentecost is Onan, and this was a demonstration of spiritual onanism; an iniquity-induced mockery of receiving the gift of the Holy Spirit. I not only observed this mockery, I experienced it, my mouth speaking the same gibberish, my body gyrating, lifting up off the floor, only to be flung into a nearby wall. This experience led to my very first revelation, on spiritual masturbation, onanism; of one's self, self-generated. The Pentecostal religion even refers to itself as the Oneness religion. The belief that one receives the Holy Ghost or Holy Spirit was one of many false beliefs accepted in the heart of this Gentile Judah.

The King that rules Judah

Jeroboam was the first king to rule Israel, revealing the contentious spirit ruling the Mind. Rehoboam, the first *king* to rule *Judah,* reveals the *spirit* ruling the *Heart.* To see how this unholy spirit rules our heart, we must look at how Rehoboam ruled the people.

> ... *My little finger shall be thicker than my father's loins. And now whereas my father did lade you with a heavy yoke, I will add to your yoke: my father hath chastised you with whips, but I will chastise you with scorpions. 1 Kings 12:10,11*

All the false religious images formed from God's Word over the past two thousand years, makes up the heavy yoke of bondage the religious peoples of the world serve under. This spiritual bondage is symbolized by the physical bondage the children served under in Egypt. The *heavy yoke* symbolizes the *oppression* that comes with accepting these false religious beliefs in the heart, so many carnal interpretations being assigned to spiritual truth. Some give reverence to a God on earth they call Father, when Jesus said, *"Call no man your father upon the earth"* Priests are oppressed by the carnal religious belief that requires them to remain celibate, which Paul advocated for, conflicting with his epistle to Timothy in which he states that in refusing to marry, one is giving heed to seducing spirits and doctrines of devils (1Timothy 4:1-3). It is this carnal-minded belief that would have many sexually frustrated priests preying upon innocent altar boys. We've allowed ourselves to be humiliated as we sat in our confessionals, believing that by exposing all of our so-called sins, we would be forgiven. Clearing the slate, along with our conscience, we would sin again, humiliating ourselves all over again at our next confession. Some look to the clouds for the return of Jesus, believing in a rapture that will take them out of the *time of trouble* that is already upon the earth. All of this religious iniquity, causing so much confusion, and adding to the spiritual flood of evilness that comes with putting our trust in these man-made images; in these false *gods*.

But where are thy gods that thou hast made thee? Let them arise if they can save thee in the time of trouble: for according to the number of thy cities are thy gods, O Judah. Jeremiah 2:28

For the vineyard of the Lord of hosts is the house of Israel, and the men of Judah his pleasant plant: and he looked for judgment, but behold oppression; for righteousness, but behold a cry. Isaiah 5:7

It is the women of Judah that demonstrate this *oppression* on the outside. They are restricted in their apparel, and any type of adornment of the face or body, is oftentimes forbidden. They are clothed in a thick veil of religious dogma, which the burqa, wore by religious women in the Middle East, symbolizes, both ruled by the oppressive spirit of Judah.

Religion has taken the spiritual Word of God and handed it over to carnal interpretations, forming false images, which have led the followers of these beliefs into spiritual stagnation and oppression.

It is the women that suffer oppression because the *woman* symbolizes *flesh,* and it is our flesh; our bodies, hearts, and minds, we oppress. These oppressive religions are manifestations of a tyrannical regime we have set up to rule us from within, which we put in power when we took the spiritual kingdoms of our mind and heart out from love and truth, and handed it over to fear and lies. We fear the lies that we ourselves have given power to.

The oppression of Rehoboam, the *king of Judah,* symbolizing the *spirit of the Heart,* exists in us all, and the ruler we have vested with absolute power is our fearful, angrily-controlled, selves. The spirit of the heart is anger, which leads to oppression, and has many of us beating our flesh into subjection, working and exercising our bodies to exhaustion in support of some false image, which we worship in exchange for a false sense of empowerment. This is not the authentic power of the heart, which the spirit of fear and humiliation stripped us of long ago, but a spurious power that brings false peace of mind. Our children suffer oppression and violence, starving their bodies and cutting their flesh, witnessing to the internal anger and pain of their heart. We fear that what we eat and drink will pollute our bodies, when Jesus makes it perfectly clear that it is not what enters our body that defiles us, but what proceeds out of our heart; the unholy spirit of anger, which works with the unholy spirit of control that feeds off the unholy fear of our mind.

The word *Rehoboam* means *a people will enlarge.* It was the tribe of Judah that enlarged among all the tribes, as it is the doctrine of Pentecost, Judah of the Gentiles that has enlarged, being accepted by the majority of mainstream Christians. Proclaiming out of the spirit of impatience that they are born again and saved, Israel and Judah have finally become one, but not for the good.

And Jehoshaphat [king of Judah] *said to the king of Israel, I am as thou art, my people as thy people, my horses as thy horses. 1 Kings 22:4*

The word *horse* means *to skip, also a swallow (from its rapid flight).* The spirit of Judah is impatience, and it is this impatience that has caused them to skip over the spiritual works or labor; skipping over the process of spiritual birth, which was foretold by the prophet Isaiah.

Before she travailed, she brought forth; before her pain came, she was delivered of a man child. Who hath heard such a thing? Who hath seen such things? Shall the earth be made to bring forth in one day? Or shall a nation be born at once? ... Isaiah 66:7,8

The scripture prophesies of a false belief that will spread throughout all of mainstream Christianity. It was Pentecost, Judah of the Gentiles that formed the belief that one could be born again without travailing. It is not possible to give birth without travailing, without tribulation; a time of trouble that many Christians still believe they will not go through. More religious iniquity, adding to the veil of flesh over the heart, which the holy seed, spiritual truth, cannot, and will not, penetrate. Is it any wonder artificial insemination and in vitro fertilization are on the rise? Our inability to conceive of seed is a manifestation of our inability to conceive of truth, and it has little to do with our age. Our eggs are old because our ideologies are old; beliefs that have caused us to become spiritually inept, beliefs that have no power to contribute to spiritual life. Man's seed is sluggish and diminished because these carnal-minded ideologies repel and destroy God's holy seed of spiritual truth. To quicken our spiritual reproductive systems, we must greatly desire truth, a love of truth that will revitalize us spiritually as well as physically.

And so it is written, The first Adam was made a living soul; the last Adam was made a quickening spirit. 1 Corinthians 15:45

The word *quickening* means *to revitalize, make alive, give life.*

As the world leaves the era of Isaac, which is associated with Judah, and enters the era of Jacob, which is associated with Zion, it is time to leave behind the mockery of God's Word. This is done by replacing the carnal interpretations assigned to scripture over millennia through the man-made doctrines of religion, with spiritual interpretation, thereby restoring the spiritual teachings of Jesus. It is time to rend the spiritual kingdom of God out of the hand of its oppressors, which have absconded with its spiritual truths. Whether she is a false religious image that has spread throughout the earth, or a false self-image that has permeated our heart, Judah has enlarged her borders, her spirit enlarging to include fear, anger, control, and impatience. These are the four earthly spirits; the four beasts or living ones that stand before the *throne,* symbolizing the *heart,* preventing us from living our authentic lives. Judah's spirit of impatience, which grows stronger and stronger with each generation, is keeping us in spiritual and physical debt as we continue to demand immediate spiritual and physical gratification. It's a spirit that is causing great mental, emotional, and physical oppression, oppressing the soul.

In your patience possess ye your souls. Luke 21:19

Judah's Judgment for Disobedience

And I beheld another beast coming up out of the earth; and he had two horns like a lamb, and he spake like a dragon. And he exercised all the power of the first beast before him, and causeth the earth and them which dwell therein to worship the first beast, whose deadly wound was healed.
Revelation 13:11,12

Our false images or beliefs may appear as harmless as a lamb, but their words, spoken into our heart, having the power to manifest, are quite deadly. When the Jews made the decision to leave Jerusalem to become merchants, they gave power to the first beast, which resulted in the death of six million, six thousand, and six, Jews. We have all made the decision to leave our divine protection by buying and selling false religious and self-images within that spiritual temple called the heart, giving power to the second beast. The second beast exercises all the power of the first beast, man's spiritual evilness added to his physical evilness. Man's spiritual disobedience is bringing forth judgment. And once again, it will be man's own spiritual *wickedness* that will correct him.

Thine own wickedness shall correct thee, and thy backslidings shall reprove thee; know therefore and see that it is an evil thing and bitter, that thou hast forsaken the Lord thy God, and that my fear is not in thee, saith the Lord God of hosts. Jeremiah 2:19

September 11th 2001, 9-11, was a serious wake-up call, one that should have brought us back into the borders of obedience. Reparation for our wrong doings will require death; death to our old way of thinking and believing. The Jews judgment came by way of a physical fire. Our judgment will come by way of a spiritual fire that will purify our hearts. A Jew is one born of Hebrew parents. The word *Hebrew* means *a region across, on the opposite side, esp. of the Jordan*; from the root word meaning *to cross over, used widely of any transition*. We make our way down to a spiritual Jordan by admitting to our fear. The fear of not only beginning the journey that will change our life in a positive and profound way, but the fear of leaving behind the false beliefs that have led us into the uncertain place in which we now find ourselves. We continue the journey by admitting to our anger, and by acknowledging that our control has had a negative effect upon us, and those around us. We will come to understand that our impatience has caused us to make a lot of wrong or bad decisions throughout our life. These are the spiritual enemies that have kept us from inheriting a joyful, abundant, and fruitful life. Fighting against these unholy internal enemies is the true meaning of a holy war. Like the Jews of the Holocaust, we will be stripped; stripped of our false images and the evil spirits that help empower them. We will offer ourselves as a living sacrifice, the flames of a spiritual judgment consuming the beast within, bringing us into a new state of being. Purified through a spiritual holocaust, we emerge as spiritual Zionists, as the Jews were purified through a physical holocaust, the last of a series of catastrophes for the Jews, which lead to a Zionist state.

> ... *The sceptre shall not depart from Judah, nor a lawgiver from between his feet, until Shiloh come; and unto him shall the gathering of the people be. Genesis 49:8-10*

The word *sceptre* means *a scion, i.e. (lit.) a stick for punishing.* As long as we remain under the spirit of Judah, we remain under its punishment, which is manifesting itself in the form of terrorism and oppression. The *feet* symbolize the *age of Pisces,* synonymous with the *era of Isaac,* and with the *reign of Judah.* We have left this era chronologically, but we will remain under its tyranny until we drive the impurities out of our heart, through which we bring in *Shiloh,* meaning *to be tranquil, secure, successful, be happy, prosper, be in safety.* Those that reach this state will have entered the Ark of the Covenant; the ark of safety, abiding in God's protection, safe from the flood of evilness that is quickly rising upon the earth, as it has risen upon the heart of man. What will it take to move us out of Judah and into Zion? It will require us to partake in a spiritual healing process, the details of which have been encoded in scripture using a symbolic code, which reveals the psychology of scripture, through which we understand the mental and emotional occurrences that have brought us into the addicted and oppressed state in which we now find ourselves. It is through this ancient code that we receive God's ancient instruction, which if followed, will deliver us of our spiritual and physical bondages. Will we allow ourselves to be caught up in this transformation process that leads to an authentic raptured state, or fight against it?

Chapter Six
Zion

Out of Israel came Judah, and out of Judah came Zion. This would be as true among the Gentiles as it was for the Jews. This is where I come in. I had come home to work during my summer break from college. It was 1975, I was twenty-three, and having the time of my life, so I was not prepared for what was about to happen. Having landed a job in the Florida Keys as a housemother for troubled boys, I was paired with a housefather, who loved to talk about God, rekindling my interest. On one of my days off, on my way home to visit with my family two hours north, I did a favor for my co-worker. He had asked me to drop off his guitar, which needed some work, so I obliged, having no idea that it would change my life, forever. As I walked into this building on the outskirts of my hometown, I noticed a scripture posted on the wall: *Acts 2:38*. And on the desk, a very big book, which piqued my curiosity. A man had acknowledged my presence, but was preoccupied and seemed to be in no particular hurry. I waited, and waited, meandering my way over to the desk where that big book was. I sat down, looked around, and then leaned over, and gingerly opened it. It turned out to be a book of Bible words, a number given for each word. Clueless, I closed the book. The man finally made his way out of his workshop. We talked about what needed to been done on my friend's guitar, and then I asked a question pertaining to the Bible, one I thought up to ask him, while waiting. What this man said so intrigued me, I ended up hanging out with him over the next couple of days, having pretty much decided, then and there, that I would not return to school in the fall. My schooling would take place here, with this man. It was a study that would last nineteen years, and I would learn all about that big book on his desk.

This man, whom I consider to be a true man of God, began his odyssey in 1960. And like me, he had no previous teachings on the Bible. In fact, from a beginner's standpoint, he knew less than I did. He once told me that when he read the first four books of the New Testament, he broke down and cried after each book. He thought Jesus kept coming back, and they kept killing him, not aware that it was the same story being told by different men. This was a pure vessel, his mind a clean slate, quiet, having no preconceived ideas about God's Word. It was in 1960 that he received a picture in his mind of a nearby church, where he was instructed to go and be baptized. It was a Pentecostal Church; Judah of the Gentiles, where he received the name through water baptism following fifty days of prayer, in which he heard things like *"the seed, the seed, the seed."* Frustrated, he would cry out, *"Lord, what about the seed?"* And with that question, the information started pouring in. What he heard he wrote down, papers I recall seeing some years after we met. He had gone through a period of repentance in those fifty days, and was baptized in the name of Jesus in accordance with *Acts 2:38,* in the church called out to bear the name. What happened to him that night in the church was readily accepted, mirroring their image of what they call *"getting the Holy Ghost,"* only this was not a mockery. This display was for the congregation, as the gift of the Holy Spirit had already been received in the form of truth he received over those fifty days. When he spoke in tongues, two in the congregation received the interpretation, after which time he was asked to teach from the pulpit. But what he taught did not support their beliefs. He was speaking things they did not understand, a new language, and it wasn't long before he and his teachings were angrily rejected.

The man of God spent the next fourteen years alone, being taught. Fifteen years from the time this man experienced a connection with the spirit of truth, which began in 1960, a new people was gathered together. Pentecost was given fifteen years in which to accept this truth, before being cut off in 1975. And what is quite interesting, is that during those *fifteen years,* a religious Jew named Yehuda, Hebrew for Judah, stayed in contact with this man of God. Judah of the Gentiles and Judah of Judaism were both privy to the spirit of truth teachings.

Turn again, and tell Hezekiah, the captain of my people, Thus saith the Lord, the God of David thy father, I have heard thy prayer, I have seen thy tears: behold, I will heal thee: on the third day thou shalt go up unto the house of the Lord. And I will add unto thy days fifteen years; and I will deliver thee and this city out of the hand of the king of Assyria; and I will defend this city for my own sake, and for my servant David's sake. 2 Kings 20:5,6

Israel, who became Judah at the crossing of the Jordan, was also given a period of fifteen; fifteen hundred years in which to assimilate this *ancient spiritual truth,* illustrated by their eating of the *old corn* in the land of Canaan, which replaced the *manna,* symbolizing the c*arnal law.* But fifteen hundred years later, when the spiritual word of God returned to take them out from the law, which they went back under through their disobedience in the Promised Land, they rejected it, wasting the holy seed, illustrated by Onan, the second son of Judah, who spilled the seed upon the ground. God then chose a new people, open-minded pagans, Gentiles, who understood the spiritual, drinking of the new wine and speaking with new tongues. When God's people stagnate by slipping back into a carnal way of thinking, a strong dose of God's spirit and word appears to move them forward into a spiritual way of thinking. If they reject it, there will be a new people prepared to take their place. God's kingdom is always moving; moving us into a deeper spiritual understanding, which if applied through action, brings us back to our place of origin. When a people refuses to move forward, they are left behind, demonstrated through the movement of planets, which occasionally go retrograde, reverting to an earlier or inferior condition. The planet appears to stop, or move backwards relative to other objects that are moving forward. Judah went retrograde, becoming as Israel, reverting to an inferior condition; without the name, as it is written, *"the latter end is worse with them than the beginning"* (2Peter 2:20). Judah of the Gentiles became worse off than Israel of the Gentiles because they received the name, but did not bring forth fruit unto God, breaking another Commandment: *"Thou shalt not take the name of the Lord thy God in vain"* Exodus 20:7

And the Lord said unto me, The backsliding Israel hath justified herself more than treacherous Judah. Go and proclaim these words toward the north, and say, Return, thou backsliding Israel, saith the Lord; and I will not cause mine anger to fall upon you: for I am merciful, saith the Lord, and I will not keep anger for ever. Only acknowledge thine iniquity, that thou has transgressed against the Lord thy God, and hast scattered thy ways to the strangers under every green tree, and have not obeyed my voice, saith the Lord. Turn, O backsliding children, saith the Lord; for I am married unto you: and will take you one of a city, and two of a family, and I will bring you to Zion. And I will give you pastors according to my heart, which shall feed you with knowledge and understanding. Jeremiah 3:11-15

Judah, Pentecost, never brought forth fruit unto God, so the name was taken away from them and given to a new people, to Zion. This Zion, gathered together in the carnal era of Isaac, went through a carnal baptism, taking on the carnal name, while Judah became as backsliding Israel, without a name, and having been married to God through a spiritual intercourse, was given a bill of divorce. This occurred in 1975, when the man of God heard the word, *Ichabod*. Having never heard the word before, much less how to spell it, he turned to that big book, Strong's Concordance of the Bible, searched through it, and found it. The word *Ichabod* means *there is no glory*. This is the story of Ichabod:

Now the sons of Eli were the sons of Belial; they knew not the Lord... Wherefore the sin of the young men was very great before the Lord: for men abhorred the offering of the Lord. 1 Samuel 2:12,17

The word *Belial* means *without profit, worthlessness, destruction, wickedness, evil, naughty, ungodly men*. These two men, who did evil by robbing God with respect to sacrifices, represent the Gentile Israel and Judah, who were cut off *in one day*, in 1975.

And this shall be a sign unto thee, that shall come upon thy two sons, on Hophni and Phineas; in one day they shall die both of them. And I will raise me up a faithful priest that shall do according to that which is in my heart and in my mind: and I will build him a sure house: and he shall walk before mine anointed for ever. 1 Samuel 2:34,35

The *faithful priest* in the story is Samuel, but spiritually, he is anyone that hears the word of the Lord, and obeys it, offering the spiritual sacrifices of God (Psalms 51:17). He is one with whom the ark resides, the two cherubims in the ark symbolizing God's spirit and word, through which we make our spiritual sacrifices. It is our holy spirit that brings our false beliefs to light, delivering the truth through which we sacrifice them, consuming them out of our life.

And the ark of God was taken; and the two sons of Eli, Hophni and Phineas were slain. 1 Samuel 4:11

The *ark* that was built in the wilderness symbolized the *power* that was with God's people, Moses embodying the Spirit of God, and Aaron, who spoke of Moses, being that he was *"slow of speech"* (Exodus 4:10), symbolizing the Word of God, the *ark of God* symbolizing the *power of the two witnesses of God*.

And his daughter in law, Phineas' wife, was with child, near to be delivered: and when she heard the tidings that the ark of God was taken, and that her father in law and her husband were dead, she bowed herself and travailed; for her pains came upon her. And about the time of her death the woman that stood by her said unto her, Fear not; for thou hast born a son. But she answered not, neither did she regard it. And she named the child Ichabod, saying, The glory is departed from Israel: for the ark of God is taken. 1 Samuel 4:19-22

Elijah's Three Incarnates

The Spirit, appearing on this earth, resting upon individual men, can be seen in the story of Elijah and the juniper tree.

And as he lay and slept under a juniper tree, behold, then an angel touched him, and said unto him, arise and eat. And he looked, and, behold there was a cake baken on the coals and a cruse of water at his head. 1 Kings 19:5

Elijah *slept,* illustrating his physical death. He arose, his spirit returned, resting upon John the Baptist, the *cake* and *cruse of water* symbolizing the *spirit* and *word* of God; John and Jesus.

When the chief baker saw that the interpretation was good, he said unto Joseph, I also was in my dream, and behold I had three white baskets on my head: And in the uppermost basket there was of all manner of bakemeats for Pharaoh; and the birds did eat them out of the basket upon my head. And Joseph answered and said, This is the interpretation thereof: The three baskets are three days. Yet within three days shall Pharaoh lift up thy head from thee, and shall hang thee on a tree...

And it came to pass that on the third day, which was Pharaoh's birthday, that he made a feast unto all his servants: and he lifted up the head of the chief butler and of the chief baker among his servants. And he restored the chief butler unto his butlership again; and he gave the cup into Pharaoh's hand: But he hanged the chief baker: as Joseph had interpreted unto them. Genesis 40:16-22

And when a convenient day was come, Herod on his birthday made a supper to his lords, high captains, and chief estates of Galilee; And when the daughter of the said Herodias came in and danced, and pleased Herod and them that sat with him, the king said unto the damsel, Ask of me whatsoever thou wilt, and I will give it thee... And she came in straightway with haste unto the king, and asked, saying, I will that thou give me by and by in a charger the head of John the Baptist... And immediately the king sent an executioner and commanded his head be brought: and he went and beheaded him in the prison. Mark 6:21-27

The *chief baker,* symbolizing the *spirit,* was cut off, which we see in the beheading of John the Baptist. But the *chief butler,* symbolizing the *word,* Jesus, continued his service, teaching the kingdom of God. *"He must increase, but I must decrease,"* which John spoke of Jesus and himself. Once the seed of spiritual truth was delivered, the spirit or energy needed to deliver it decreased as it became one with the seed, which increased, becoming energized seed, which could now be conceived of within the heart of man through spiritual obedience, bringing forth good fruit unto God.

And the angel of the Lord came a second time, and touched him, and said, Arise and eat; because the journey is too great for thee. And he arose, and did eat and drink, and went in the strength of that meat for forty days and forty nights unto Horeb the mount of God.
1 Kings 19:7,8

Elijah arose for the second time, his spirit returning. One can't help but make the connection between this story and

Moses' story. He goes to *Horeb*, where he witnessed God's Spirit in the burning bush. He then leads the children of Israel to the mount of Sinai, another name for Horeb, where he spends *forty days and forty nights* receiving the Law of God. But we need to go forward in time, not backward, bringing the return of God's Spirit closer to those living today, in what is the end of days. The Spirit of truth returned in 1960, bringing the teachings to Judah, of the Gentiles, and of the Jews, both of which rejected them. Fifteen years later, the spiritual ark moved, taking the name with it, making Judah like her sister, Israel. Israel, Catholic and Trinity, was more justified than Judah, Pentecost, because the more truth we receive, the more we are held accountable for our actions. Elijah *went in the strength of that meat forty days and forty nights,* representing forty years. The *meat,* symbolizing *spiritual truth,* would take forty years to be processed, made ready for consumption, coinciding with the new millennium. On the third and final return, again the spirit rested upon one man, through whom the *"spirit of truth"* rested upon a new people; upon the type and shadow daughters of Zion, in the carnal era of Isaac. We are now in the third and final era of Jacob, the spiritual era, in which God's spirit and word, the spirit of truth, will come to rest upon the individual (John 16:13); upon the spiritual daughters of Zion, whose desire to heal has activated the holy spirit of their heart, the power needed to complete the spiritual works of God's word, which results in the revitalization of the holy spirit and the regeneration of the word of truth; the resurrection of the two witnesses of the heart, through which their spiritual life is restored to its former glory, returned to the condition in which they received it from God upon their birth.

And after three days and an half the Spirit of life from God entered into them, and they stood upon their feet; and great fear fell upon them which saw them. Revelation 11:11

"One day is with the Lord as a thousand years." It has been thirty-five hundred years since the Spirit and Word, embodied in Moses and Aaron, came to retrieve the children of Israel out of the bondage of Egypt. Now it's our turn! We have always had the ability to resurrect the two internal witnesses of our heart. It's been going on since the beginning of God's dealing with man, by those who have cleared their minds of preconceived ideas, allowing their portion of God's holy spirit to bring them into the light of truth. But only recently has the resurgence of spirit begun to take place on a much larger scale, on a global level.

Now Eli was ninety and eight years old; and his eyes were dim, that he could not see. And the man said unto Eli, I am he that came out of the army. And he said, What is there done, my son? And the messenger answered and said, Israel is fled before the Philistines, and there hath been also a great slaughter among the people, and thy two sons also, Hophni and Phineas, are dead, and the ark of God is taken. And it came to pass, when he made mention of the ark of God, that he fell from off his seat backward by the side of the gate, and his neck brake, and he died: for he was an old man, and heavy. And he had judged Israel forty years. 1 Samuel 4:15-18

Oftentimes, the ages given in the Bible correlate with the year of our calendar. This is one of those times. The ark is being transferred from Israel to the land of the Philistines, where it brings down the image of Dagon. That is the job of our holy spirit— to bring us the truth that will bring down whatever daggone images we have erected in our heart. The word *Philistines* goes to the root meaning *to roll (in dust)*, the *dust* symbolizing *inactivity* with respect to God's spirit and word. In nineteen *ninety and eight* (1998), the antiquated idea that spirit was something that existed outside of oneself, and could only be tapped into if one associated themselves with the God of religion, *died.* What took the place of this *old* idea was the concept that spirit is something that has always been part of us, but has been forgotten and must be remembered. Out of one person's ability to set aside her fear of reprisal, would come our teachers; those who had been prepared ahead of time to guide us into a greater understanding of our spiritual essence. Global awareness of our internal holy spirit began in August of 1998 through one that had the means to bring it to the masses.

The ark being moved at the birth of Ichabod illustrated the glory of the Lord departing from Israel, and Judah, who became as Israel. This took place on a small scale in 1975 due to the perpetual *mockery* of this Gentile Israel and Judah. But now it is taking place on a universal scale. As the world leaves the era of *Isaac* and enters the third and final era of Jacob, we are given one last opportunity to leave behind our mockery or pretense, which is a false appearance or action intended to deceive, a mere show without reality; faith without works. We each have an opportunity to retrieve our spiritual ark out of *Obed-Edom* and bring it into the *city of David*, Zion, grouped with the era of Jacob, which the world entered with the new millennium. Jacob was called Israel.

We choose Jacob over Esau, which is Edom (Genesis 36:8), when we choose to get real with regard to the condition of our life. Desiring change, we begin the spiritual process through which we become Israel. Not the Israel of Judaism or Christianity; but a new Israel, a spiritual Israel, which we become not just by thinking spiritually about the Word of God, which is to drink of the spiritual drink, but by accepting the word of God into our heart through spiritual works; through spiritual obedience, which is to eat of the spiritual meat (1 Corinthians 10:3,4).

And they set the ark of God upon a new cart... So David went and brought up the ark of God from the house of Obed-Edom into the city of David with gladness. 2 Samuel 6:3,12

The *ark of God* is set upon *a new cart,* symbolizing *a new knowledge and understanding* of the Spirit and Word of God, providing us with the ancient instruction, that when followed, brings us into the *city of David;* into the kingdom of God within. *Obed-Edom* means *worker of Edom*, meaning *red*, synonymous with *Esau,* which we will address at the end of this chapter.

I bring near my righteousness; it shall not be far off, and my salvation shall not tarry: and I will place salvation in Zion for Israel my glory.
Isaiah 46:13

Salvation is in Zion.

Ah sinful nation, a people laden with iniquity, a seed of evildoers, children that are corrupters: they have forsaken the Lord, they have provoked the Holy One of Israel unto anger, they are gone away backward. Isaiah 1:4

Isaiah describes Judah.

Except the Lord of hosts had left us a very small remnant, we should have been as Sodom, and we should have been like unto Gomorrah.
Isaiah 1:9

The daughters of Zion are the *very small remnant,* a type of which appeared among the Jews as a result of the Holocaust and among the Gentiles in 1975. But now, in what is the spiritual era of Jacob, a daughter of Zion is anyone that comes out of Judah; out of *iniquity,* for which Sodom, and Gomorrah, was destroyed. The daughters of Zion, chosen out of the Gentile nation, were kept hidden. People passed through on occasion, but for the most part, we were known to no one. This was probably intended for our protection. But what we could not be protected from was our own minds and hearts. Like Israel and Judah before us, we went on to build false images. We knew enough not to buy into the false doctrines of the Christian religion, but we erred nevertheless by looking at certain things with a carnal mind, which God hates. How many times I heard the teacher say, *"you have to see that you are Judah,"* which for me began in the spring of *97,* two and a half years after the teachers death, at which time I began to pour over my notes from our Bible studies. And what I discovered was, the name I received through water baptism had been blotted out, along with my recollection of that very important fact. God has a standard, which he does not deviate from. If there is no potential for fruit to be brought forth, what need is there for the name. Like Judah, I had taken the name in vain. As I continued to peruse my notes, I made another startling discovery in those dated *11/2/92.*

> "If you plant a seed in the earth and it doesn't produce, it's because the ground is lacking something. Something needs to be removed— the -ites...

The -ites is an abbreviation for the seven nations the children of Judah were to drive out of the Promised Land, which represent the spiritual impurities of the heart (Proverbs 26:25, Matthew 15:19). The heart symbolizes the spiritual womb, which must be made pure for the sowing of God's seed of truth. My heart lacked purity.

> Scrape the ground clean, get rid of carnal things..."

On *11/4/92,* two days after having written these notes, I suffered a miscarriage, and a DNC was performed. I realized years after the fact that this was no coincidence. I remember at the time asking the teacher why this had happened. What did it mean? What could I take out of this very painful experience? He told me that this is what would happen if God sowed his seed in us now, the physical revealing the spiritual.

Give them, O LORD: what wilt thou give? give them a miscarrying womb and dry breasts. Hosea 9:14.

As difficult as this experience was at the time, it helped to know that it at least held some spiritual meaning. Thinking back on this painful experience years later, I found myself calculating the age at which I conceived. I was forty years and six months old. Again, no coincidence, as it took a period of forty and six to build the temple in Jerusalem. The *temple* symbolizes the *heart,* the spiritual womb, which if polluted, aborts God's holy seed.

Moreover the Lord saith, Because the daughters of Zion are haughty, and walk with stretched forth necks and wanton eyes and mincing as they go, and making a tinkling with their feet: Therefore the Lord will smite with a scab the crown of the head of the daughters of Zion, and the Lord will discover their secret parts... and she being desolate shall sit upon the ground. Isaiah 3:16,17,26

To be *of Zion* we must first realize that we are Judah, which takes place when we realize that we only thought we were serving God, or thought we were doing the right thing. But now we realize it was just a pretense. We begin to see that the way we are thinking and managing our life is no longer working for us, that it is only bringing us more problems. We are ready for change. In this humbled state, we make our way down to a symbolic Jordan. Here we begin the process of being stripped, our *secret parts* exposed through awareness of our false perceptions and beliefs. When we are ready to deal with the reality of our life, we become a daughter of Zion, building upon an awareness of our true condition, which we will change through works. The word *Zion* goes to the unused root meaning *to parch, aridity, a desert, barren, solitary place, wilderness.* It is a solitary place because we are the only ones that can change the way we think and feel, and what we believe. Each of us must do our own spiritual works, becoming a barren wilderness by drying up to our old way of thinking, and by sacrificing the destructive beliefs born of painful emotions. To be a spiritual daughter of Zion takes work, but it is worth it!

And though the Lord give you the bread of adversity and the water of affliction, yet shall not thy teachers be removed into a corner anymore, but thine eyes shall see thy teachers: And thine ears shall hear a word behind thee, saying, This is the way, walk ye in it, when ye turn to the right hand, and when ye turn to the left. Ye shall also defile the covering of thy graven images of silver, and the ornament of thy molten images of gold: thou shalt cast them away as a menstruous cloth; thou shalt say unto it, Get thee hence. Isaiah 30:20-22

The Holocaust, where they ate the *bread of adversity* and drank of the *water of affliction,* served as the Jews transition from Judah to Zion. The *silver* in the graven images of silver symbolizes the *fear* that empowers the lies of our mind. The *gold* in the molten images of gold symbolizes the *purity* we have attributed to these false beliefs or images, the high value we place on them demonstrated through our actions, which stand in support of them, empowering them. Out of adversity and affliction will come our teachers as we cry out in our time of trouble, learning, through the holy power of the heart, what false images or beliefs we have bought and sold within that spiritual temple called the heart. In overcoming these destructive beliefs, we enter back into God's protection, as the Jews made their way back into Jerusalem. The Holocaust, through the power of the first beast, completed the Jews transition from Judah to Zion. The second beast, which exercises the same power as the first beast, will accomplish the same end, moving us from Judah into Zion, from sorrow into joy.

Whenever we make a decision to change our life for the better, we can count on some adversity and affliction, as

Israel encountered hurdles in the wilderness upon leaving Egypt. But if we hang in there, do the works, and don't get impatient, we will see our teachers, which will feed us with knowledge, knowing for a surety that we have made the right decision. We will hear that inner voice speaking through our holy spirit, telling us that we are moving in the right direction. We will have begun our spiritual journey, casting away the false perceptions created in fear, lies generated by the false images or beliefs that are being empowered by the hidden anger of our heart. As a daughter of Zion, we ascend through levels of self-awareness.

And in that day seven women shall take hold of one man, saying, We will eat our own bread and wear our own apparel: only let us be called by thy name, to take away our reproach. Isaiah 4:1

The number *seven* pertains to the *spiritual;* to the spiritual process. To *take hold of one man* is to *take hold of truth.* We do this by eating of the *bread,* symbolizing the process of *overcoming* our false beliefs, through which we are clothed in spiritual *apparel,* the spiritual wedding garment that is *truth*, which is the *name.*

He that hath an ear, let him hear what the Spirit saith unto the churches: To him that overcometh will I give to eat of the hidden manna, and will give him a white stone, and in the stone a new name written, which no man knoweth saving he that receiveth it. Revelation 2:17

The *hidden manna* is synonymous with the bread. It is hidden because it is not something you see, but rather something you think and feel. The *white stone* symbolizes the *righteous word* of God. And like the new apparel, *a new name* symbolizes *a new truth,* one diametrically opposed to the error we empowered through our old, untruthful thoughts and beliefs. Only he who receives this new truth knows it, experiencing it through the positive and constructive changes taking place in his life since accepting this new truth into his heart. For those that make the decision to change their life by leaving a church, one whose religious doctrine is governed by the oppressive spirit of Judah, a word of warning! In expressing what you are seeing and hearing to those that are content to remain in the limitations of religious thinking, you risk the chance of being hated and rejected by them, because that's the spirit of Judah, the spirit you will be leaving behind as you go through this healing process, leaving behind the spirit of self-hatred and rejection. You are in the process of leaving Judah to enter Zion, the *city of David*, meaning *to get your eyes open to Love*, and YOU will be the first recipient of that love.

These things I command you, that ye love one another. If the world hate you, ye know that it hated me before it hated you. If you were of the world, the world would love his own, but I have chosen you out of the world, therefore the world hateth you. Remember the word that I said unto you, The servant is not greater than his lord. If they persecuted me, they will also persecute you; if they have kept my saying, they will keep yours also. But all these things they will do unto you for my name's sake, because they know not him that sent me. If I had not come and spoken unto them, they had not had sin: but now they have no cloke for their sin. He that hateth me, hateth my Father also. But this cometh to pass, that the word might be fulfilled that is written in their law, They hateth me without a cause. John 15:17-25

If you are a member of a fundamentalist church or legalistic synagogue, and choose to drink of the new wine, which is to think spiritually about the Word or Law of God, do not be dismayed when you are driven out. And it is not that you will be physically removed, or even asked to leave. What will drive you out now, in the spiritual era of Jacob, are the spirits of those that are not yet willing to open their ears that they might hear, and their eyes that they might see. That transition is going to require a bit more tribulation on their end!

These things have I spoken unto you, that ye shall not be offended. They shall put you out of the synagogues: yea, the time cometh, that whosoever killeth you will think that he doeth God service. And these things will they do unto you, because they have not known the Father, nor me.

John 16:1-3

Killing in the name of religion has been going on for millennia, as one self-righteous fanatical group after another sets out to kill anyone that refuses to believe the same way they do. But for the most part, for now anyway, this death will be spiritual, as those close to you remove you out of their lives as if you were dead.

Those that do the spiritual works of bringing down the false self-images or beliefs that they have been holding onto since childhood will discover the self-hatred and rejection that has been emanating from within. They will fight against these destructive influences through the power of their holy spirit; the spiritual energy that brings to light the false word or belief that's been empowering this self-hatred and rejection. Through this transformation process, they will remove the evil seeds; the negative and destructive beliefs, making way for the good seed or word of truth, which will spring up to everlasting life; a good life, one filled with the good fruits of the spirit, which lasts forever.

And the daughter of Zion is left as a cottage in a vineyard, as a lodge in a garden of cucumbers, as a besieged city. Isaiah 1:8

The word *cucumber* comes from the unused root meaning *to be hard, the cucumber (from the difficulty of digestion)*. For some it might be hard to digest the fact they have been worshipping false images. For others it might be difficult to digest the rejection they feel from those they once considered friends because they have chosen to drink of the spiritual drink and eat of the spiritual meat in this spiritual era.

And one shall say unto him, What are these wounds in thine hands? Then he shall answer, Those with which I was wounded in the house of my friends. Zechariah 13:6

And for others still, it may be the process itself that is hard to accept, because it either conflicts with what they have been taught about salvation, or because it is different than anything they've experienced in the past. It helps to keep in mind that those that are coming against you are in a place of fear, too afraid to let go of something familiar in order to experience something new. This was the case with the children of Israel, who were afraid to traverse the wilderness, and ascend the mount. We are afraid to let go of our old ways, not trusting that there's a better life ahead. Afraid to take a chance on something that we don't know the outcome of, which is a lack of faith. *"Do something, even if it's wrong,"* the teacher said. And looking back, I realize he said those words because he knew the day would come when we would have to challenge the fear of our mind with action; with works that prove and perfect our faith. If it turned out I had made a huge mistake, I could swallow my pride, and crawl back, but that was not to be the case. I left behind a mental bondage, one of my own choosing, to enter a new land; a new way of life, in which I would find incredible freedom. Shortly after leaving behind this place of limitation, upon waking one morning, I heard, *"Rachab,"* which I immediately looked up. It means *roomy, in any or every direction, at liberty, to broaden.* When I told my friend, who had left the group two years prior to my leaving, what I had heard, and the meaning of the word, she said that David set his feet in a large room, quoting from the book of Psalms.

I will be glad and rejoice in thy mercy: for thou hast considered my trouble; thou has known my soul in adversities. And hast not shut me up into the hand of the enemy: thou hast set my feet in a large room.
Psalms 31:7,8

There is nothing to fear. Trust that inner voice that is moving you on. It won't be long before you begin to see the fruits of your labor— a more joyful and fulfilling life, one filled with a lot less stress.

In that day shall the branch of the Lord be beautiful and glorious, and the fruit of the earth shall be excellent and comely for them that are escaped of Israel. And it shall come to pass, that he that is left in Zion, and he that remaineth in Jerusalem, shall be called holy, even everyone that is written among the living in Jerusalem. Isaiah 4:2,3

The *excellent and comely* fruit is that of your holy spirit, which you will bring forth as you overcome the works of the flesh. The works of the flesh are actions taken out of fear, anger, hatred, bitterness, resentment, etc., all generated from living to these false beliefs that have taken up residency in our heart. *Zion* refers to the process by which we purify our mind and heart. We purify our heart by driving out its unholy inhabitants, sanctifying our temple. And once our temple is made holy through righteous truth, our thoughts will be right, healthy thoughts, which our body following will demonstrate through positive and constructive actions. *Jerusalem* refers to the new Jerusalem atop mount Zion, symbolizing a new peaceful state, obtained through the spiritual works of a spiritual judgment (Psalms 122). To be *of Israel* is to escape or be saved from all of our false beliefs, becoming holy, becoming spiritual Israel.

And so all Israel shall be saved: as it is written, There shall come out of Zion the Deliverer and shall turn away ungodliness from Jacob. For this is my covenant unto them, when I shall take away their sins.
Romans 11:26,27

The word *saved* means *deliver, protect, heal, save (self), be (make) whole*. What we are saved or delivered from through God's ancient healing process is the sin that is keeping us from becoming spiritually whole; the error that keeps us from being healed in mind, heart, and body; in thought, emotion, and action, the three aspects of the soul. The earth is leaving the era of Isaac, which coincides with the age of Pisces. Those that move with this transition leave behind the spirit of Judah, with its energy of delusion, a pretentious spirit that possesses one with a feeling of euphoria. This spirit gives the mind false peace, which acts as a wall, keeping the painful and hidden feelings of the heart from penetrating the mind. The spirit of Judah is being perpetuated by doctrines that teach us to repent, which is to think differently, but not to change or transform the heart, through which the negative and destructive energy of the earth is being generated. New Age Christians call anything that can be construed as negative and destructive, an illusion, denying the existence of evil. Believing evil does not exist only gives it power. Denying it only keeps one from seeing it in their self. These mainstream and new age doctrines act as a wall of flesh, preventing one from seeing the impurities of his heart. But if they are courageous enough to let go of these false doctrines, they will enter the era of Jacob, becoming a daughter of Zion, going through a process that will deliver them of their sin, which has been hiding in the darkness of denial. If we refuse to admit that our life is not all that we would like it to be. And then do the internal work that will make our life what we want it to be, we remain as Esau, who dwells in mount Seir.

Thus dwelt Esau in mount Seir: Esau is Edom. Genesis 36:8

The word *Seir* means *tempestuous, rough,* describing our life when we choose to remain deluded. Esau forfeited his birthright for *red pottage,* which translates to *dangerous arrogance.* To claim that we are born again and saved or already spirit and perfected before we have completed the spiritual works through which we enter this state, is pure arrogance. This dangerous religious belief has spread throughout Christianity;

its origins tracing back to Pentecost, which is Edom. To claim we are spirit before we have gone through the process that brings on the birth of the spirit from within, is detrimental to the healing of the soul. Anyone who is not getting real about their less-than-perfect life is forfeiting their spiritual birthright, their right to a perfected life. *Jacob* refers to those that choose to do the spiritual, mental and emotional, work that will make their life joyful and abundant. This will require them to humble themselves to a process that will change their lives, delivering them of all of their false beliefs. It is the process of overcoming the negative aspects of the twelve sons of Jacob, which being the twelve tribes of Israel, are neither lost nor extinct, but existing within. Through this spiritual process or judgment, we reach that perfected or ascended state that many are claiming out of delusion, spiritual laziness, and impatience.

And many people shall go and say, Come ye, and let us go up to the mountain of the Lord, to the house of the God of Jacob; and he will teach us his ways, and we will walk in his paths; for out of Zion shall go forth the law, and the word of the Lord from Jerusalem. Isaiah 2:3

The *mountain* and *house* symbolize the *heart*. The *law* is *love* and the *word* is *truth*, the two witnesses of the heart, through which we complete our spiritual works, and enter our *rest*.

For the Lord hath chosen Zion; he hath desired it for his habitation. This is my rest forever: here will I dwell; for I have desired it.
Psalms 132:13,14

And saviours shall come up on mount Zion to judge the mount of Esau; and the kingdom shall be the Lord's. Obadiah 1:21

The word *saved* means *deliver, protect, heal, save (self), be (make) whole*. The *saviours* are those that are saving themselves through christ; through the healing power of the heart. When the salvation process is complete, the kingdom is the Lord's, love and truth ruling the mind and heart. This purified and perfected state is called Zion.

Chapter Seven
Babylon

The word *Babylon* means *confusion*, a derivative of the word Babel. We enter this world in accordance with God's Creation, filled with God's spirit of love and His word of truth. But in the process of time, we separate ourselves from this pure spiritual essence, building a spiritual tower of Babel, brick by brick, lie by lie, the carnal mind carrying us away into Babylon; into confusion.

And the whole earth was of one language, and of one speech, And it came to pass, as they journeyed from the east, that they found a plain in the land of Shinar; and they dwelt there. And they said one to another, Go to, let us make brick, and burn them thoroughly. And they had brick for stone, and slime had they for mortar. And they said, Go to, let us build us a city and a tower, whose top may reach into heaven; and let us make us a name, lest we be scattered abroad upon the face of the earth. And the Lord said, Behold the people is one, and they have one language; and this they begin to do: and now nothing will be restrained from them, which they have imagined to do. Genesis 11:1-6

In the beginning, we had one language, and that language was truth. But in the process of time, we imagined what we would, the word *imagined* meaning, *to plan, usually in the bad sense, think (evil)*. We went from having good, positive and constructive, right thoughts to having evil, negative and destructive, wrong thoughts. We *journeyed from the east,* leaving the presence of God, departing from God's spirit and word by replacing love and truth with fear and lies; the mortar and bricks that gave strength to the false beliefs symbolized by this brick tower.

Go to, let us go down, and there confound their language, that they may not understand one another's speech. So the Lord scattered them abroad from thence upon the face of all the earth: and they left to build the city. Therefore the name of it is called Babel; because the Lord did there confound the language of all the earth: and from thence did the Lord scatter them abroad upon the face of the earth. Genesis 11:7-9

The word *confound* means *to cause to become confused*, which has come about through our different languages, the *us* that confounded the language of religion were the two witnesses of spirit and truth, *"the spirit of truth."* When Martin Luther received a portion of truth, which was rejected by the Catholic Church, he broke away, building a new church, with a new language. Each religion has a fraction of truth, the religious image, as it stands today, having only two elevenths, encoded in the story of Micah, whose mother took two hundred of the eleven hundred shekels to build the image (Judges17). The number eleven represents the fullness of God, which the religious image falls greatly short of. There are as many religious languages as there are religious images or beliefs, each religious faction imagining what they will.

Thou, O king, sawest, and behold a great image. This great image, whose brightness was excellent, stood before thee; and the form thereof was terrible. This image's head was of fine gold, his breast and his arms of silver, his belly and his thighs of brass, His legs of iron, his feet part of iron and part of clay. Thou sawest till that a stone was cut out without hands, which smote the image upon his feet that were of iron and clay, and brake them to pieces. Then was the iron, the clay, the brass, the silver, and the gold, broken to pieces together, and became like the chaff of the summer threshing floors; that no place was found for them: and the stone that smote the image became a great mountain, and filled the whole earth. Daniel 2:31-35

The *head of gold* symbolizes the doctrine of the Catholic Church. The *breasts* and *arms of silver* symbolize the doctrine of Trinity. The *belly* and *thighs of brass* symbolize the doctrine of Pentecost. The *legs of iron* symbolize the *political power* that gives strength to the religious image. The *feet, part iron and part clay*, symbolizes the mixing of politics and religion. This was the image seen by the *king of Babylon*, which translates to the *spirit of confusion*.

Thou, O king, art a king of kings; for the God of heaven hath given thee a kingdom, power; and strength, and glory... thou art this head of gold.
Daniel 2:37,38

The great religious image that has brought so much confusion was headed by the Catholic Church, the Mother Church...

And upon her forehead was a name written, MYSTERY, BABYLON THE GREAT, THE MOTHER OF HARLOTS AND ABOMINATIONS OF THE EARTH. Revelation 17:5

And after thee shall arise another kingdom inferior to thee and another third kingdom of brass, which shall bear rule over all the earth.
Daniel 2:39

The second kingdom, inferior in power to the Catholic Church, is Trinity. But it is the third kingdom, Pentecost, whose spirit of anger and oppression will *bear rule over all the earth*. The first two kingdoms make up Israel, symbolizing the Mind, the gold and silver revealing the spirits that are ruling the mind. The word *gold* means *yellow*, symbolizing *doubt*, yellow being the slang word for *cowardly*. The word *silver* means *to become pale, fear*. Doubt and fear are ruling the mind. But it is the third *kingdom of Judah*, symbolizing the *realm of the Heart* that is our real concern. The negative and destructive spirit ruling the heart is of *brass*, which means *the red color of the throat of a serpent when hissing.* The color *red,* in this context, symbolizes *danger,* the *hissing serpent* symbolizing the *anger* that brings with it great oppression, a threatening spirit that will bear rule over the whole earth.

And the fourth kingdom shall be strong as iron: forasmuch as iron breaketh in pieces and subdueth all things: and as iron that breaketh all these, shall it break in pieces and bruise. Daniel 2:40

After this I saw in the night visions, and behold a fourth beast, dreadful and terrible, and strong exceedingly; and it had great iron teeth: it devoured and brake in pieces, and stamped the residue with the feet of it: and it was diverse from all the beasts that were before it; and it had ten horns. Daniel 7:7

The *fourth kingdom* is synonymous with the *fourth beast,* which is *diverse* in that it is political; dreadful, terrible, and strong. The *ten horns,* like the ten toes, symbolize *ten political kingdoms* or *nations* that give their power to the beastly religious image.

And whereas thou sawest the feet and the toes, part of potter's clay, and part of iron, the kingdom shall be divided; but there shall be in it the strength of the iron, forasmuch as thou sawest the iron mixed with the miry clay. And as the toes of the feet were part of iron and part of clay, so the kingdom shall be partly strong, and partly broken. And whereas thou sawest iron mixed with miry clay, they shall mingle themselves with the seed of men: but they shall not cleave one to another, even as iron is not mixed with clay. Daniel 2:41-43

The *clay* symbolizes the *religious image,* the *iron* symbolizing the *political power* that gives strength to the beastly religious image, the two kingdoms *divided* through separation of church and state. They have mingled with the seed of men from generation to generation, yet they shall not cleave one to another, maintaining a degree of separation. The political nations of today, united in power, are contributing to this dreadful oppressive spirit, giving strength to the beastly religious image by failing to do what it takes to overtake it. The greatest weapons of mass destruction are not atomic, chemical, or biological, having the power to destroy the body. The greatest weapons of mass destruction are the beliefs of oppressive religions, having the power to destroy the body and the soul.

The *ten toes* in the image symbolize *ten kings* that have power to rule the people by mixing politics and religion, one World Government and one World Religion. Both government and religion have become corrupt, the rulers seeking external power, motivated by monetary and spiritual greed, the root of all the evil we are facing in the world today. As long as we, the people, continue to support these false religious beliefs, which rule through the politics of fear, anger, and control, we will continue to be oppressed, losing the freedom we have fought so hard to preserve. To take the power away from corrupt governments and oppressive religions, we must remove the source empowering them, which is coming from within; through *ten kings,* symbolizing *ten spirits.*

And in the days of these kings shall the God of heaven set up a kingdom, which shall never be destroyed: and the kingdom shall not be left to other people, but it shall break in pieces and consume all these kingdoms, and it shall stand forever. Daniel 2:44

The *days of these kings* represent the days in which religious kingdoms are supported by political kingdoms, which began two thousand years ago, and continues to this very day. It is in the days of these carnal kings and kingdoms, that the *God of heaven* establishes a kingdom that is set up within the individual, which can never be destroyed. It is not *left to other people* because it is spiritual, following the builder of such a kingdom into the spiritual realm. Those that seek this internal kingdom will bring to an end the three inferior kingdoms of gold, silver, and brass through an internal process. To see how this is done, we must look at the covenant God made with Abram.

After these things the word of the Lord came unto Abram in a vision, saying, Fear not, Abram: I am thy shield, and thy exceedingly great reward. And Abram said, Lord God, what wilt thou give me, seeing I go childless, and the steward of my house is Eliezer of Damascus? And Abram said, Behold to me thou hast given no seed: and, lo, one born in my house is my heir. And, behold, the word of the Lord came unto him, saying, This shall not be thine heir; but he that shall come forth out of thine own bowels shall be thine heir. And he brought him forth abroad, and said, Look now toward heaven, and tell the stars, if thou be able to number them: and he said unto him, So shall thy seed be. And he believed in the Lord; and he counted it to him for righteousness. And he said unto him, I am the Lord that brought thee out of Ur of the Chaldees, to give thee this land to inherit it. And he said, Lord God, whereby shall I know that I shall inherit it? And he said unto him, Take me a heifer of three years old, and a she-goat of three years old, and a ram of three years old, and a turtledove, and a young pigeon. And he took unto him all these, and divided them in the midst, and laid each piece one against another: but the birds divided he not. Genesis 15:1-10

Abram has no seed. He has yet to bring fruit unto God. His heir is Eliezer of *Damascus,* symbolizing *death and destruction.* The word *Eliezer* means *God of help,* which comes through the ancient spiritual knowledge that provides the instruction for getting rid of our inheritance of death and destruction and receiving our inheritance of life and peace. This will come through our own *bowels,* meaning *the seat of generation,* which spiritually, is the heart. Life and peace will come through the regeneration (Matthew 19:28); through the truth we regenerate in that spiritual throne called the heart. The *heifer, she-goat,* and *ram* are *three years old,* representing the past *three thousand years.*

It was in the beginning of these three thousand years, that a lamb, one without spot or blemish, was put on the altar and sacrificed. That lamb, Jesus, brought man the spiritual instruction that was to be used to divide the heifer, she-goat, and ram, preparing them for sacrifice. But man refused. And now, in what is the beginning of the last of these days or years (2 Peter 3:8), man is given one more opportunity to atone for the death of innocence that has taken place within, and without. It was on the third day that the children of Israel were to climb the mount, illustrating our journey through the heart. It was on the third day that the water was turned to wine, symbolizing the people that are being turned to spirit through their sacrificing of a beastly spiritual flesh.

And it came to pass, that, when the sun went down, and it was dark, behold a smoking furnace, and a burning lamp that passed between those pieces. Genesis 15:17

The *furnace* symbolizes the spiritual *judgment* that will consume our beastly sacrifice, the *lamp* symbolizing the *light of truth* that exposes the heifer, the she-goat, and the ram.

And the great city was divided into three parts, and the cities of the nations fell:.. Revelation 16:19

The *great city* is Babylon. The word *city* means *to have your eyes opened,* and what we are to have our eyes opened to is our own confusion. To bring down Babylon, we must divide the heifer. The word *heifer* goes back to the root word meaning *to revolve, circular,* as the children of Israel went around in circles in the wilderness, symbolizing the *patterns* we keep repeating. We will break these *cycles* when we divide the she-goat. The word *she-goat* means, *to be stout,* or *stubborn,* a characteristic of the astrological goat. It is stubbornness that keeps us going around and around in these same old habits. Stubbornness, which boils down to fear and doubt or lack of trust, keeps us from getting to the truth, which frees us from the beliefs that cause us to repeat the same mistakes. Truth divides the ram. The word *ram,* means *strength* in the negative sense. The *ram* symbolizes *idolatry,* the worshipping of false images. We have been using the power of our false religious and self-images or beliefs to fight against the truth. The *turtledove* and *pigeon* symbolize *repentance,* and the process of being *plucked clean,* stripped of our covering of filth, which comes from harboring the *foul* spirits that empower the false beliefs that make up the beastly image seen by the king of Babylon.

And he cried mightily with a strong voice, saying, Babylon the great is fallen, is fallen, and is become the habitation of devils, and the hold of every foul spirit, and a cage of every unclean and hateful bird.
Revelation 18:2

Our desire to sacrifice these three, in this third day, lifts up our holy spirit, symbolized by the *"iron,"* which *"breaketh in pieces and subdueth all things."* When these three are overcome from within, we come out of spiritual darkness to begin our climb up the mount, passing through levels of light; levels of awareness, overcoming the seven nations that inhabit our spiritual promised land. The *nations* of Babylon, which fall through this purification process, are spiritual nations, spiritual inhabitants that are to be driven out of our heart.

In the same day the Lord made a covenant with Abram, saying, Unto thy seed have I given this land, from the river of Egypt unto the great river, the river Euphrates: The Kenites, and the Kenizzites, and the Kadmonites, And the Hittites, and the Perizzites, and the Rephaims, And the Amorites, and the Canaanites, and the Girgashites, and the Jebusites. Genesis 15:18-21

These ten nations are synonymous with the ten toes of the image, which are part clay and part iron, symbolizing the false image and the power behind it. To bring down the false image, we will have to use the strength of the iron. Not the inferior iron of the false image, but the superior iron of the true image, our holy spirit, which breaks in pieces and subdues by exposing the false image through the light of truth that destroys it. By dividing the heifer, the she-goat, and the ram, we weaken the head, arms, breast, belly, and thighs of the great image, the weight of which brings us to our knees, down to a spiritual Jordan, where we begin the spiritual works of fighting against and overcoming these unholy *nations* that inhabit our spiritual promised land. The heifer, she-goat, and ram; the gold, silver, and brass, along with the iron and the clay, are overcome through the *works* of the first four churches in the book of Revelation.

And to him that overcometh, and keepeth my works unto the end, to him will I give power over the nations: And he shall rule them with a rod of iron; as the vessels of a potter shall they be broken to shivers: even as I received of my Father. Revelation 2:26,27

Jesus finished his works, completing his own transformation process, using the power and strength he gained through his works to teach us the ancient instruction for spiritual purification, which has been brilliantly encoded in scripture. The *vessels of a potter* symbolize the *false images we have molded* throughout our life. These dishonorable vessels or beliefs, the beast within, are destroyed by the power of the two witnesses; through the power of the *rod of iron;* the holy spirit, and the spiritual works of God's Word.

And the ten horns which thou sawest are ten kings... these have one mind, and shall give their power and strength unto the beast.
Revelation 17:12,13

The *ten horns* or *ten kings* symbolize *ten spirits,* which work through the mind, given power to the false beliefs of the heart.

... Till thou sawest that a stone was cut out without hands, which smote the image upon his feet that were of iron and clay, and brake them to pieces. Then was the iron, the clay, the brass, the silver, and the gold, broken to pieces together, and became like the chaff of the summer threshing floors; and the wind carried them away, that no place was found for them: and the stone that smote the image became a great mountain, and filled the whole earth. Daniel 2:34,35

The *stone* symbolizes *truth,* which brings down the great image associated with the king of Babylon; with the spirit of confusion. This truth becomes *a great mountain* which fills the *whole earth,* symbolizing the *whole heart;* our whole being, in the face of which no false image or belief can ever stand.

This is how the process works. You come into the awareness that something in your life is not as it should be. You see that you keep going around and around in circles, repeating the same patterns or mistakes in your life. At some point, you realize there is a reason you keep repeating these patterns, and that you have been fighting against admitting those reasons, to yourself. Finally, you realize that you are stuck in these cycles because of some belief, some false image you have formed. This awareness is the lamp passing between the heifer, the she-goat, and the ram. With this new awareness, you are determined to do something about it. This determination is the desire that activates your kingdom of iron, raising up your holy spirit, as it is written, *"and the iron did swim"* (2 Kings 6:6). Through this power, you fight against the remnant of these unholy nations that exist within you. Overcoming these nations brings us further and further into the light of truth; further and further out of the darkness of confusion; out of Babylon.

On the morning of April 10th 2001, I heard upon waking: *Jeremiah. Read. Uzziah, Jotham, Ahaz, and Hezekiah. We are in the days of Hezekiah.*

Hezekiah, sick unto death, was given fifteen years to set his house in order. (Isaiah 38:1-5). Mankind is spiritually in the same condition as Hezekiah. And as Judah of Judaism and Judah of the Gentiles, who were given fifteen hundred and fifteen years respectively, we are given a spiritual period of fifteen to get our spiritual house in order.

The word of the Lord that came to Jeremiah concerning all the people of Judah... Because you have not obeyed my words, Behold I will send and take all the families of the north, saith the Lord, and Nebuchadnezzar the king of Babylon, my servant, and I will bring them against this land, and against the inhabitants thereof, and against all these nations round about, and will utterly destroy them, and make them an astonishment, and an hissing, and perpetual desolations. Jeremiah 25:1,8,9

The world entered Judah, synonymous with the era of Isaac, two thousand years ago. We are the people of that era; *the people of Judah*. For over fifteen hundred years people have chosen religious iniquity over spiritual truth. Every one of us has chosen lies over truth. Our spiritual disobedience is now bringing forth judgment, coming in the form of destruction from the north, even as the region of Judah in Jerusalem today has enemies coming from the north. This time of trouble, both physical and spiritual, will bring with it, the *king of Babylon;* the spirit of confusion, so that we begin to question our beliefs, and put an end to the death and destruction that is being perpetuated by the ten unholy nations that exist within, which support the *beast,* symbolizing the *false religious and self-images* we have given power to. Jeremiah, Judah's last prophet, told Zedekiah, Judah's last king that the people of Judah were to submit to the king of Babylon and serve him seventy years, after which time they would return to the holy city Jerusalem. It will take a spiritual period of seventy to bring us out of the city of Babylon, and into the city of Jerusalem.

Seventy weeks are determined upon thy people and upon thy holy city, to finish the transgression, and to make an end of sins, and to make reconciliation for iniquity, and to bring in everlasting righteousness, and to seal up the vision of the prophecy, and to anoint the most Holy.
Daniel 9:24

Judah was given *seventy* years to assimilate truth. It is through a spiritual measure of seventy that we tear down the spiritual beastly image, within.

And I stood upon the sand of the sea, and saw a beast rise up out of the sea, having seven heads and ten horns, and upon his horns ten crowns, and upon his heads the name of blasphemy. Revelation 13:1

We overcome the *ten* powers that rule us from within by going through *seven* levels of *spiritual* (mental and emotional) *awareness— 10 x 7=70*. As we come to the end of the kingdom of Judah by entering the final era of Zion, we come to the last of the kings of Judah, Zedekiah, who is told, by the prophet Jeremiah, to submit to the king of Babylon, which is to admit to the spirit of confusion; admit we are confused. This humble state brings us down to a symbolic Jordan, where we begin the spiritual judgment through which our lies are replaced with truth, bringing us out from the spirit or captivity of confusion, fulfilling our seventy years.

But Zedekiah would not heed Jeremiah's advice. He refused to submit to the king of Babylon, which would have saved his life, the life of his people, and Jerusalem. Zedekiah's eyes were put out, and he was carried into Babylon where he died in prison. In refusing to admit to our confusion we are left blinded to the truth, bound by our prison of lies, iniquity, or sin, the wages of which is death; death with regard to the full potential of our soul. We are going into Babylon, whether we go willingly or forced by the circumstances of our reality.

Therefore hearken not unto the words of the prophets that speak unto you, saying, Ye shall not serve the king of Babylon: for they prophesy a lie unto you. Jeremiah 27:14

Will we continue to listen to our mind, which is feeding us lies, telling us we are not confused? We are the people of Judah, dwelling in Babylon, in bondage to confusion until we admit we are confused, which is our ticket to begin the journey that delivers us out of the city of Babylon and into the holy city, *new Jerusalem,* symbolizing a *new peaceful state,* in which we find joy, freedom, and true peace. Following the death of Zedekiah, *Gedaliah,* meaning *Jah has become great,* is made governor. If we heed the words of Gedaliah, we will complete the process through which Jehovah is magnified within us. Like the stone that became a great mountain, we will increase in truth.

And Gedaliah sware to them, and to their men, and said unto them. Fear not to be the servants of the Chaldees: dwell in the land, and serve the king of Babylon; and it shall be well with you. 2 Kings 25:24

The *Chaldees* are the inhabitants of Chaldea, a land that worshipped images. Abram dwelt in this land until he became aware that he was serving images, and not God. We must not be afraid to see that we have been worshipping images that have made us a slave to confusion, which again, is illustrated in the lamp passing between the heifer, the she-goat, and the ram. To be delivered of the confusion brought on by our false religious and self-images we have to admit that we have them, and understand that we have been serving them through our belief in them, which we demonstrate through actions that support them.

And I saw another sign in heaven, great and marvellous, seven angels having the seven last plagues; for in them is filled up the wrath of God. And I saw as it were a sea of glass mingled with fire: and them that had gotten the victory over the beast, and over his image, and over his mark, and over the number of his name, stand on the sea of glass, having the harps of God. Revelation 15:1,2

The *seven angels* are *spiritual messengers,* which speak to us through the messages encoded in the *seven last plagues.* These plagues come to get us moving, out of bondage and into freedom, as they did with the children of Israel. The *fire* symbolizes the *judgment* through which we overcome the *beast, his image,* and *his mark,* which is the destruction that follows the beastly image. When we overcome the beast of false beliefs, we stand on a *sea of glass,* symbolizing our ability to *see through* these beliefs.

And the sixth angel poured out his vial upon the great river Euphrates; and the water thereof dried up, that the ways of the kings of the east might be prepared. Revelation 16:12

So Jeremiah wrote in a book all the evil that should come upon Babylon... When thou comest to Babylon, and shalt see it, and shalt read all these words; Then shalt thou say, O Lord, thou has spoken against this place, to cut it off, that none shall remain in it, neither man nor beast, but that it shall be desolate for ever. And it shall be, when thou hast made an end of reading this book, that thou shalt bind a stone to it, and cast it into the midst of the Euphrates: And thou shalt say, Thus shall Babylon sink, and shall not rise from the evil that I will bring upon her: and they shall be weary. Thus far are the words of Jeremiah. Jeremiah 51:60-64

The *river Euphrates* symbolizes *a river of wasteful thoughts*; negative and destructive thoughts that have been repressed, hidden in the depths of our mind, separating us from the painful emotions we have suppressed in our heart, causing an internal struggle.

And the children struggled together within her; and she said, If it be so, why am I thus: And she went to enquire of the Lord. Genesis 25:22

When we cry out from our heart, questioning our undesirable state or situation, as the children of Israel cried out because of their bondage in Egypt, we are admitting that we are confused, entering Babylon. This cry, the sounding of the *seventh angel,* opens the seventh seal or seventh chakra, activating the divine spiritual energy that will bring us into the light of truth as to the true state of our heart. It is through the light of truth that we are delivered out of spiritual darkness; out of spiritual Babylon— out of confusion.

But in the days of the seventh angel, when he shall begin to sound, the mystery of God should be finished, as he hath declared unto his servants the prophets. And the voice which I heard from heaven spake unto me again, and said, take the little book which is open in the hand of the angel which standeth upon the sea and upon the earth.
Revelation 10:7,8

The *mystery of God* pertains to the *kingdom of God;* the *Heart* (Mark 4:11), which is where *"Mystery Babylon the Great"* rules. But for those whose life has been opened up through the *seventh angel,* which stands upon the *sea* and the *earth,* symbolizing the connection between the *hidden thoughts* of the mind and the *heart,* the mystery is finished.

And I went unto the angel, and said unto him, Give me the little book. And he said unto me, Take it, and eat it up; and it shall make thy belly bitter, but it shall be in thy mouth sweet as honey. And I took the little book out of the angel's hand, and ate it up; and it was in my mouth sweet as honey: and as soon as I had eaten it, my belly was bitter. And he said unto me, Thou must prophesy again before many peoples, and nations, and tongues, and kings. Revelation 10:9-11

The *little book* symbolizes *our life,* in which we ate of good and evil. When we first took an untruthful thought into the *mouth* of our *mind,* it was *sweet,* having no immediate negative consequence. But when we ate of it, accepting it into the *belly* of our *heart* through painful emotions, it became *bitter,* as the fall-out for accepting this false word or belief in our heart would be wrong choices, which led to grief, and misery.

Thy way and thy doings have procured these things unto thee; this is thy wickedness, because it is bitter, because it reacheth unto thine heart. My bowels, my bowels! I am pained at my very heart; my heart maketh a noise in me; I cannot hold my peace... Jeremiah 4:18,19

The word *bitter* means *to be moved with choler,* one of the four humors or liquids of the body that in the Middle Ages was thought to cause anger and bad temper when present in excess. When we realize that it was our anger and false beliefs that caused us to crucify the truth of our heart, we should find it impossible to separate ourselves from those that pierced Jesus' side, leaving a bitter taste in our mouth. The word *bitter* also means *to fix a peg, through the idea of piercing.* Jesus experienced this bitterness at his crucifixion when he was given gall mixed with vinegar to drink. Gall is liver bile, and the *liver* is the seat of anger. And so it is no coincidence that Mary, the mother of Jesus, Mary, the sister of Martha, and Mary Magdalene were present at the death of Jesus. Mary comes from *Marah,* meaning *bitterness, angry, discontented, be sorely grieved,* describing our emotional state when the truth is crucified in our heart.

For the king of Babylon stood at the parting of the way, at the head of the two ways, to use divination: he made his arrows bright, he consulted with images, he looked in the liver. Ezekiel 21:21

The *king of Babylon* or *spirit of confusion* exists within all of us. Those that admit to this confusion will begin a spiritual process that will open up the seven seals of the book of their life, revealing the mystery by revealing the well-hidden thoughts and memories of the mind and the false beliefs and painful emotions of the heart. These beliefs have made our heart one of anger, and our life one of bitterness. Those that do the spiritual works required to identify and overcome these false images or beliefs will be healed. Through their personal testimonies, and by being living examples of positive change, they will help others. But those that refuse to admit to their confusion, adhering to beliefs that do not require them to enter their heart, whereby they sustain a false mind-peace, will retain their angry, their bitterness rising up when the plagues of the earth force them into *Babylon;* into *confusion.* When the truth, the reality of what is taking place in the world, fails to agree with the *iniquity* of the religious image that was sold to them, they will become very confused. And having to admit they were wrong is going to expose their anger, and their bitterness.

... know therefore and see that it is an evil thing and bitter, that thou hast forsaken the Lord thy God... Jeremiah 2:19

The Iniquity & Confusion Regarding Jesus

...and they shall see the Son of man coming in the clouds of heaven with power and great glory. Matthew 24:30

This is a spiritual event, which takes place immediately after our tribulation or personal time of trouble, upon the spiritual darkening of our symbolic sun and the moon, taking place in the *clouds of heaven,* symbolizing the *thoughts of the mind.*

And when he had spoken these things, while they beheld, he was taken up: and a cloud received him out of their sight. Acts 1:9

Jesus was taken up, a cloud receiving him *out of their sight,* meaning, they did not see him taken.

And while they looked steadfastly toward heaven as he went up, behold, two men stood by them in white apparel; Acts 1:10

The *two men* in white apparel symbolize the *two witnesses,* who in that day were John the Baptist and Jesus the Christ; the embodiments of God's Spirit and Word of God; the *"spirit of truth,"* which has come to guide the men of Galilee into the truth regarding Jesus' return.

Which also said, Ye men of Galilee, why stand ye gazing up into heaven? this same Jesus, which is taken up from you into heaven, shall so come in like manner as ye have seen him go into heaven. Acts 1:11

If the men of Galilee were doing right by gazing up into heaven, what need would there have been for the two men to question it? The two witnesses of God have come to correct their thinking, to stop the iniquity regarding a physical return of Jesus, who will come in the same manner as he left, *out of their sight,* a return not seen!

There will be no physical return of Jesus. His second coming took place two thousand years ago, his first being his birth. The third coming is spiritual, coinciding with the third spiritual era of Jacob, in which Jesus returns to the individual, in the spiritual form of truth returning to his heart.

And as for the prophet, and the priest, and the people, that shall say, The burden of the Lord, I will even punish that man and his house... And the burden of the Lord shall he mention no more: for every man's word shall be his burden; for ye have perverted the words of the living God... Jeremiah 23:34,36

Christians say, *The burden of the Lord* by saying Jesus died for their sins, their sins expunged through "the blood of Christ," more religious iniquity. The truth is Jesus died because of our sins; because of our iniquities (Isaiah 53:5). Truth dies because of iniquity, not in place of it. The burden is not the Lord's. The burden is ours to carry. Jesus carried the cross to illustrate the burden that man's word of *iniquity* has laid upon the truth. Those that do not carry their own burden by doing the works of overcoming their word of false religious beliefs will experience the consequence of that choice, which will not be pleasant. Christians are *in the midst of Babylon;* in the midst of the confusion caused by the *iniquity* of this external Babylon called the Church.

Flee out of the midst of Babylon, and deliver every man his soul: be not cut off in her iniquity; for this is the time of the Lord's vengeance; he will render unto her a recompense. Jeremiah 51:6

Chapter Eight
Jerusalem

Jerusalem (*Yerushalayim*), a city, the capital of Israel, which is comprised of the old Jerusalem and the new Jerusalem. The wall of Jerusalem has twelve gates, consistent with the twelve openings on the female body. The wall of Jerusalem symbolizes our physical flesh body. Whether we are born male or female, our body, being made of a woman, is female in gender. This is the law of God, as it is written, *"God sent forth his Son, made of a woman, made under the law."* Jerusalem symbolizes *the Heart.*

The wall of Jerusalem serves to protect the temple, as the wall that is the flesh body serves to protect the heart. The physical heart gives life to the physical body. But it is the state of the spiritual heart, our emotional state that determines our life expectancy. The ark of covenant dwells inside the inner room of the sanctuary, as the holy spirit and word of truth, male, dwells in the inner room of the mind; in the heart, female, which determines the life and form of our ethereal or spiritual body. The male is the inner being and the female is the flesh, as it is written, *"male and female created he them."*

Jesus answered and said unto them, Destroy this temple, and in three days I will raise it up. Then said the Jews, Forty and six years was this temple in building, and wilt thou rear it up in three days? But he spake of the temple of his body. John 2:19-21

It takes a little over forty weeks, 40 and 6, or 40.06, to build the physical temple or body. But the temple that is to be raised on the third day, which the world entered with the new millennium, is the spiritual temple. Resurrection is of the dead. So how can the spiritual temple be raised while the physical temple or body still lives? Through a spiritual death. To understand what must die, if not the flesh body, we must look at the spiritual meaning of the city of Jerusalem, the capital of Israel; the official seat of government. *Israel* is governed by *Jerusalem*. The *Mind* is governed by the *Heart*. It is what dwells inside the spiritual Jerusalem that must die.

Israel is my son, even my firstborn. Exodus 4:22

Reuben, thou art my firstborn... Genesis 49:3

Israel symbolizes the *mind,* and *Reuben* symbolizes the *spirit of the mind.* Reuben defiled his father's bed by lying with *Bilhah,* meaning *to palpitate, to terrify.* We defile the chamber of the holy spirit, our heart, when our mind intercourses or communicates with the unholy spirit of fear. It was the fear of the mind that prevented the children of Israel from ascending the mount. They remained at the foot of mount Sinai, worshipping the image of a false god, forming the flesh that was the carnal mind, the *veil* over Moses' face symbolizing the invisible *sinful flesh* that kept them from seeing, and hearing (obeying) the spiritual Law of God. This flesh, the carnal mind, is *bondage.* Jerusalem symbolizes the Heart, of which there are two states: bondage and free; *Hagar* and Sarah. The children of Israel remained in *bondage* to the carnal Law. They represent the Jerusalem that is in bondage.

For this Hagar is mount Sinai in Arabia, and answereth to Jerusalem which now is, and is in bondage with her children. Galatians 4:25

Note: The Hebrew word for Jerusalem (*Yerushalayim*) contains the root word *-ayim*, meaning *fright, to frighten, an idol [as a bugbear]:- dread, fear, horror, terrible, terror.*

The terrorism in the world today is being generated by the terror that exists within each and every one of us; a destructive fear buried so deep in the psyche that most of us are not yet aware of its existence.

The 12 gates in the wall of Jerusalem symbolize the 12 aspects found in the 12 sons of Jacob or the 12 tribes of Israel. These aspects, positive and negative, determine the type of wall, astral to abject, that serves to protect what is in the heart. The body, outermost Jerusalem, obeys the mind, transitory Jerusalem, which obeys the heart, innermost Jerusalem. The heart is the throne; we are ruled by our emotions. If we allow fear, an emotion that works through our mind, to keep us disconnected from the deeper emotions of our heart, we will retain their negative energies. If we allow false peace and denial, which are fear based, to separate us from our true feelings, the anger of our heart will remain, and we will continue to rule ourselves with oppression; with an excessive or lack of control with regard to our actions. Whatever rules the heart, rules the subconscious and conscious mind, which we will demonstrate through the actions of our body. To change our behavior, we must change our heart. If we do not go on into perfection by purifying our heart, we will have to control these negative and destructive behaviors through laws we institute through our mind, for the rest of our lives.

For it is written that Abraham had two sons, the one by a bondmaid, the other by a freewoman. But he who was of the bondwoman was born after the flesh... Galatians 4:22,23

There are two Jerusalems; two Mothers. The mother exemplifies protection. One mother keeps us in bondage by protecting our word of error. The other mother keeps us free by protecting our word of truth. Abraham took Hagar before Sarah, as Jacob took Leah before Rachel. *Hagar* and

Leah symbolize the *bondage of flesh*. *Sarah* and *Rachel* symbolize the *freedom of spirit*. We must deal with our bondage in order to be free. Jacob had twelve sons, the twelve tribes of Israel, which the twelve gates in the wall of Jerusalem, represent. The number *twelve* represents *judgment,* and judging the negative aspects of the *ten* sons by Leah and the bondwomen, symbolizing flesh and bondage, formulates to *12x10,* which equals *an hundred and twenty (120)*.

And the Lord said, My spirit shall not always strive with man, for that he also is flesh: yet his days shall be an hundred and twenty.
Genesis 6:3

And Moses was an hundred and twenty years old when he died…
Deuteronomy 34:7

The *flesh* formed by our word of error, which keeps us in bondage, dies at *an hundred and twenty* by overcoming the negative aspects of the first ten sons of Jacob. *Moses* symbolizes the *Spirit* of God, but the backside of the spirit is the *law,* as it is written, *"And I will take away mine hand, and thou shalt see my back parts." Exodus 33:23.* The children of Israel would see the law, which they brought upon themselves by resisting the *Spirit,* which they illustrated by resisting *Moses.*

But if ye be led of the Spirit, ye are not under the law. Galatians 5:18

The ten sons of Leah and the bondwomen rose up against Joseph and threw him in a pit, a story that is allegorical. These sons symbolize the negative aspects that sustain the flesh that keeps us in bondage by separating us from the truth, which Joseph symbolizes. This *flesh* fights against the *spirit* that brings the truth that makes us free.

For the flesh desires the contrary of the Spirit, and the Spirit the contrary of the flesh… so you do not perform the things which you wish.
Galatians 5:17 (Greek Diaglott)

The Destruction of Jerusalem

And Jesus went out, and departed from the temple: and his disciples came to him for to shew him the buildings of the temple. And Jesus said unto them, see ye not all these things?... There shall not be left here one stone upon another, that shall not be thrown down. Matthew 24:1,2

Jerusalem was destroyed in 70AD, as it is written, *"seventy years in the desolations of Jerusalem." Daniel 9:2*. The word *seven* means *to be complete*. An indefinite number, the destruction of our spiritual Jerusalem of bondage complete when we overcome the *ten* sons, which formulates to *7 x 10,* which equals *seventy*. Even the wall of Jerusalem, our physical body, is given seventy years. Any extended time is called grace. If our sin remains, so too will the spiritual flesh it forms inside of our physical flesh, so that when our final circumcision takes place at our physical death, removing the foreskin that is our flesh body, we will find ourselves wrapped in this sinful flesh, seeing ourselves as *naked* in the spiritual realm.

And the Lord called unto Adam, and said unto him, Where art thou? And he said, I heard thy voice in the garden, and I was afraid, because I was naked; and I hid myself. And he said, Who told thee that thou was naked: Has thou eaten of the tree, whereof I commanded thee that thou shouldest not eat? Genesis 3:9-11

Adam was afraid because he ate of the evil by accepting the lie into his heart, which formed a covering of sinful flesh.

Unto Adam also and to his wife did the Lord make coats of skins, and clothed them. Genesis 3:21

I counsel thee to buy of me gold tried in the fire, that thou mayest be rich; and white raiment, that thou mayest be clothed, and that the shame of thy nakedness do not appear... Revelation 3:18

The *gold tried in the fire* symbolizes *purification through the spiritual judgment* (Matthew 19:28), which removes this sinful flesh. The *white raiment* symbolizes the *word of truth*, the spiritual wedding garment one is clothed with through this purification process. We must enter that spiritual temple called the heart, and drive out its unholy inhabitants. This spiritual eviction process is the desolation of our Jerusalem of bondage. The word *Jerusalem* means *founded peaceful,* but what kind of peace has man been seeking, and protecting?

And the temple was filled with smoke from the glory of God, and from his power; and no man was able to enter into the temple, till the seven plagues of the seven angels were fulfilled. Revelation 15:8

No man can enter the *temple,* symbolizing the *heart,* until the last plague is fulfilled from within. The seventh plague is *hail,* meaning *to lower (as into a void),* bringing down the wall of our old Jerusalem of bondage so that we can see into our heart. The word *Jerusalem* means *founded peaceful,* but what kind of peace has man been seeking, and protecting? The *wall* that Ezekiel speaks of in the following verse symbolizes *false peace*, obtained through doctrines or disciplines that change the mind, but not the heart. It is the hidden emotions and beliefs of our heart that influence the thoughts of our mind on a subconscious level, driving our behaviors. If we want to bring balance to what is out of control, without having to control it through the power of our mind, which is being under a law, we must bring down the wall of false peace that is preventing us from entering into our heart to discover what is hidden there.

Because, even because they have seduced my people, saying, Peace; and there was no peace; and one built up a wall, and lo, others daubed it with untempered mortar: Say unto them which daubed it with untempered morter, that it shall fall: there shall be an overflowing shower: and ye, O great hailstones, shall fall; and a stormy wind shall rend it. Lo, when the wall is fallen, shall it not be said unto you, Where is the daubing wherewith ye have daubed it. Therefore thus saith the Lord God; I will even rend it with a stormy wind in my fury; and there shall be an overflowing shower in mine anger, and great hailstones in my fury to consume it. So will I break down the wall that ye have daubed with untempered morter, and bring it down to the ground, so that the foundation thereof shall be discovered, and it shall fall, and ye shall be consumed in the midst thereof: and ye shall know that I am the Lord. Thus will I accomplish my wrath upon the wall, and upon them that have daubed it with untempered morter, and will say unto you, The wall is no more, neither they that daubed it; To wit, the prophets of Israel which prophesy concerning Jerusalem, and which see visions of peace for her, and there is no peace, saith the Lord God. Ezekiel 13:10-16

There is no peace in the city of Jerusalem because *there is no peace* in the Heart of man. There are only visions of peace; an illusion of peace generated through the deception of a mind that has yet to connect with the heart. The war in the Middle East is evidence that man has not obtained peace in his heart. There is still a conflict that has yet to be resolved; the external revealing the internal, the physical revealing the spiritual. The Earth symbolizes the Heart. There will be no peace in the Earth until there is peace in the Heart. That it's an anagram is probably not a coincidence.

Our disorders, addictions, and diseases are all witnessing to man's decaying state, his fall into ruin. Modern medicine can't keep up with the rate of disintegration. Surgeries and drugs keep us alive and functioning, but they can also shore up this wall of false peace if we don't dig down into the heart and discover what brought on the infirmity to begin with. We began to build this wall of bondage early on in our life when we started replacing love with fear and truth with lies. Our mind devised a way to separate us from our heart; from the pain that resulted from the negative things we saw, heard, felt, and experienced. This wall of separation gave us peace of mind, and for a time, it served us well. But at some point, which for many of us will be mid-life, the holy spirit of our heart goes into crisis, our false word of false beliefs becoming a burden; a cross we can no longer bear the weight of (Jeremiah 23:36). It is then that we will begin the process of dying a spiritual death, which begins when we no longer live to the false peace that is currently keeping us from entering that spiritual temple called the heart.

Jesus, when he had cried again with a loud voice, yielded up the ghost. And, behold, the veil of the temple was rent in twain from top to bottom; and the earth did quake, and the rocks rent. Matthew 27:50,51

The veil stands between the *worldly sanctuary*, symbolizing the *mind*, and the *Holiest of all*, symbolizing the *Heart*. The *veil*, like the wall, symbolizes the *false peace* that keeps us separated from our heart; from the emotions and beliefs carrying the negative and destructive energy. The veil gives way when the *earth quakes;* when we are shaken up on a deep emotional or heart level.

And I beheld when he had opened the sixth seal, and, lo, there was a great earthquake... Revelation 6:12

On September 12th, 2001, I heard upon waking, *"This is the opening of the sixth seal,"* referring to the events of September 11th, 2001. On this day we were shaken, our heart trembling with strong emotion, rolling away the stumbling stone of false peace. We were to make our way into the innermost Jerusalem, fighting against the internal enemies that keep us from obtaining the freedom associated with the new Jerusalem; a new state obtained through spiritual sacrifices of the heart (Psalms 51:17), not through the carnal sacrifices (Isaiah 1:11-15), not through any action of the mind or body; not through prayer, tithing, baptism, anointing, fasting, etc. Not by keeping carnal laws, or by performing any other mind-body discipline. This new state can only be achieved through the purification of the heart. We must set aside practices that put us into altered states of consciousness, setting aside beliefs that serve only to establish a false peace of mind; a transitory peace that creates an illusion of peace, the veil or wall that separates us from our heart, where we will complete or finish our *works,* establishing true peace, dwelling in the free Jerusalem.

Be watchful, and strengthened [be strong about] *the things which remain, that are ready to die: for I have not found thy works perfect before God.*
Revelation 3:2

The word *perfect* means *to complete, to finish.*

Create in me a clean heart... renew a right spirit within me. Cast me not away from thy presence; and take not thy holy spirit from me. Restore unto me the joy of thy salvation; and uphold me with thy free spirit... The sacrifices of God are a broken spirit: a broken and a contrite heart... Do good in thy good pleasure unto Zion: build thou the walls of Jerusalem.   Psalms 51:10-12,17,18

Through the spiritual sacrifices of God, we revitalize our holy spirit and regenerate our word of truth, overcoming the fear and lies that kept us in bondage. We will live free, protected inside *the walls of Jerusalem;* inside the walls of the new spiritual Jerusalem.

And Jesus said unto them. Verily I say unto you, That ye which have followed me, in the regeneration when the Son of man shall sit in the throne of his glory, ye also shall sit upon twelve thrones, judging the twelve tribes of Israel.   Matthew 19:28

The number *twelve* represents *judgment.* Judging the negative aspects of the twelve tribes of Israel formulates to *12 x12,* which equals *an hundred and forty and four (144),* the measure of the wall of the new Jerusalem, a spiritual measure man reaches through the completion of his six (metaphorical) days of (spiritual) works, which formulates to *6 x 24,* which equals *144.*

And he measured the wall thereof, an hundred and forty and four cubits, according to the measure of a man, that is, of the angel.
Revelation 21:17

Him that overcometh will I make a pillar in the temple of my God, and he shall go no more out: and I will write upon him the name of my God, and the name of the city of my God, which is new Jerusalem...
Revelation 3:12

The *new Jerusalem* symbolizes a *new peaceful state,* which we obtain through the creation of *a new heaven and a new earth,* symbolizing *a new mind and a new heart,* a state that once entered into, one will never leave.

And I saw a new heaven and a new earth: for the first heaven and earth were passed away; and there was no more sea... no more death, neither sorrow, nor crying, neither shall there be any more pain: for the former things are passed away. Revelation 21:1,4

There is *no more sea* because the thoughts or memories hidden in the darkness of denial or repression, no longer exist, having been brought to light through the transformation process. There is *no more death* because the spiritual death is complete. There is no more *sorrow, nor crying, neither any more pain* because the painful emotions of the heart have passed away, along with the false beliefs that generated them. Peace has been established within.

Jerusalem is builded as a city that is compact together: For there are set thrones of judgment, the thrones of the house of David. Pray for the peace of Jerusalem: they shall prosper that love thee. Peace be within the wall, and prosperity within thy palaces. For my brethren and companion's sakes, **I will now say, Peace be within thee.** *Because of the house of the Lord our God I will seek thy good. Psalms 122:3,5-8*

Chapter Nine
The Great Tribulation

Our tribulation or *time of trouble* is as individual as a woman's delivery. No two will be exactly the same. The purpose of tribulation is to get us to let go of whatever it is that is keeping us from becoming our true selves, and manifesting our true desires. It can come in any number of ways, appearing as internal unrest, or manifesting as physical pain or disease. Our tribulation may be the result of the loss of a loved one, or the result of financial difficulty. Its intensity depends upon the degree of pressure it takes to be *delivered*. Some deliveries are easy, others quite difficult. Some come with great pain, others nearly painless.

And at that time shall Michael stand up, the great prince which standeth for the children of thy people: and there shall be a time of trouble, such as never was since there was a nation even to that same time: and at that time thy people shall be delivered, everyone that shall be found written in the book. Daniel 12:1

It is in times of difficulty that we learn about ourselves; an opportunity to reveal what has been hidden in that spiritual womb called the heart.

Behold, I was shapen in iniquity; and in sin did my mother conceive me. Behold, thou desirest truth in the inward parts: and in the hidden part thou shalt make me to know wisdom. Psalms 51:5,6

Our tribulation might be emotional, felt through fear, anxiety, anger, depression, loneliness, bitterness, resentment, etc. These feelings rise up to show us something is wrong. Those not prone to masking or running away from their feelings will deal with them early on. As soon as they feel troubled from within, they set out to discover why, and when they are shown, they take care of it promptly, and completely, making for a quick delivery. But those that fight against the process of spiritual birth will have a more difficult time. If the emotional pain that has been bottled up within us is not allowed to come to light and be transformed, it will move out, felt as pain in the body, or show up in the form of a cyst or tumor. It may manifest as a disorder of the mind or a disease of the body, whatever it takes for us to become introspective, to look inside of ourselves. If we ignore our spiritual healing at this time, healing the outside only, we will most likely find our infirmity returning, taking on the same form, or choosing a new form, all for the purpose of healing our emotions, the seat of the soul.

The body's ability to materialize the negative and destructive energy of the soul in the form of disease is a demonstration of God's love and compassion. Cancer is sin materialized; one eating away at our physical life as the other eats away at our spiritual life. It is no coincidence that laser light is being used in the treatment of cancer, as the word *laser* is compared with *lazar*, one *afflicted with disease,* from *Lazarus*. Physical light has the power to restore the body, but the spiritual light of truth has the power to restore the body and the soul. The light of truth puts sin in remission by transforming its negative and destructive energy. Now positive energy, it moves out, healing the body by changing its chemical composition, changing the physiology of our organs, tissues, cells, etc. Disease is the result of a separation from God, a departure from God's spiritual Law.

...If thou wilt diligently hearken to the voice of the Lord thy God, and wilt do that which is right in his sight, and will give ear to his commandments, and keep all his statutes, I will put none of these diseases upon thee, which I have brought upon the Egyptians: for I am the Lord that healeth thee. Exodus 15:26

Egypt symbolizes the *World.* We are the *Egyptians,* our diseases a result of the negative and destructive energy being stored within. The plagues of Egypt are allegorical; a tribulation or time of trouble that got the children of Israel motivated to leave behind the bondage of Egypt. It is going to take quite a bit of tribulation to motivate those that have accepted beliefs that have veiled them with the illusion of peace. Many so-called Christians claim they will not go through the tribulation, saying they have already given birth, that they are already born again, having given birth before they have experienced, and surmounted the pain that is part of the spiritual birthing process.

The Untimely Birth

Before she travailed, she brought forth; before her pain came, she was delivered of a man child... Shall the earth be made to bring forth in one day? Or shall a nation be born at once?... Isaiah 66:7,8

Many will come to realize that they are not born again, and that there is no deliverer coming to take them out of the tribulation that is coming upon the earth. When they renounce these false beliefs, they can begin the spiritual works or labor of spiritual birth. But some will fight against the process to the very end, never giving birth to their true selves, their names never written in the Lamb's book of life (Revelation 21:27).

And they said unto him, Thus saith Hezekiah, This day is a day of trouble, and of rebuke, and of blasphemy: for the children are come to the birth, and there is not strength to bring forth. Isaiah 37:3

The *children* are those *unskilled* in the spiritual Word of God, having no understanding of the process of spiritual birth. Having omitted the spiritual works or labor, they are spiritually weak. We are in the days of Hezekiah; in the *day of trouble* that brings on the spiritual birth (Daniel 12:1). But those who brought forth through the delusion of their mind instead through the reality of the heart will not have the *strength* to deliver. They are Esau, selling their spiritual birthright for a mess of *red pottage;* because of a *dangerous arrogance.*

And I beheld when he had opened the sixth seal, and lo, there was a great earthquake; and the sun became black as sackcloth of hair, and the moon became as blood; And the stars of heaven fell unto the earth, even as a fig tree casteth her untimely figs, when she is shaken of a mighty wind. Revelation 6:13

The opening of the *sixth seal,* in the physical, began on September 11th 2001, the beginning of the *great earthquake* that will shake the whole earth; shaking up the earthly people.

...YET ONCE MORE I SHAKE NOT THE EARTH ONLY, BUT ALSO HEAVEN. *Hebrews 12:26*

The earth symbolizes the heart. It is the beginning of a time of trouble that will shake the heart of mankind, bringing on a resurrection of truth from within the heart as many begin to turn inward. As the tribulation intensifies, it will reach into the heaven, shaking up those that have entered a heavenly state through beliefs that promised them an external salvation, or provided them with a type of peace rendered powerless in times of emotional crisis. The *untimely figs* symbolize *those that have not reached spiritual maturity,* being out of phase with God's timing due to beliefs that gave them false peace. The *mighty wind* symbolizes the *power of the holy spirit,* which will shake them up, preparing them for the coming of the Lord; the coming of truth.

Blow ye the trumpet in Zion, and sound an alarm in my holy mountain: let all the inhabitants of the land tremble: for the day of the Lord cometh, for it is nigh at hand ... Joel 2:1

The *holy mountain* symbolizes the *heart.* The sound of the *trumpet* means *prepare for battle;* the battle against the *unholy inhabitants* of the heart.

But in those days, after that tribulation, the sun shall be darkened, and the moon shall not give her light. And the stars of heaven shall fall, and the powers that are in heaven shall be shaken... Mark 13:24-27

Immediately after the tribulation of those days shall the sun be darkened, and the moon shall not give her light, and the stars shall fall from heaven, and the powers of the heaven shall be shaken: Matthew 24:29

...Behold, I have dreamed a dream more; and, behold, the sun and the moon and the eleven stars made obeisance to me... and his father rebuked him, and said unto him, What is this dream that thou hast dreamed? Shall I and thy mother and thy brethren indeed come to bow down ourselves to thee to the earth? Genesis 37:9,10

The lights of heaven symbolize the perceptions of the mind, coming through the sun, moon, and stars. The *sun* symbolizes our *father.* The *moon* symbolizes our *mother.* The *stars* symbolize our *siblings* and anyone else that influenced our thinking throughout our life. The darkening of the sun, moon, and stars is essential to the birthing process. The erroneous perceptions we received through these three sources, will be eclipsed by the light of truth as we go through God's healing process.

Fear none of those things which thou shalt suffer: behold, the devil shall cast some of you into prison, that ye may be tried; and ye shall have tribulation ten days: be thou faithful unto death, and I will give thee a crown of life. Revelation 2:10

The *devil* symbolizes *error in thinking,* holding us in a spiritual prison. The *ten days* are associated with the spiritual birthing process, as the ten centimeters reached in the physical birthing process. The *death* is twofold. The first is the death of the flesh formed by our word of error. The second is the death of our flesh body. When the flesh formed by our false word is removed through a spiritual death, we become pure spirit in essence. Upon our physical death, we will be born of that pure spiritual essence, born again, born from above, receiving a *crown of life,* symbolizing *the life we inherit* upon both our spiritual and physical deaths; a life of eternal joy, our reward for judging the negative aspects of the twelve tribes of Israel, or twelve sons of Jacob.

Because thou hast kept the word of my patience, I also will keep thee from the hour of temptation, which shall come upon all the world to try them that dwell upon the earth. Revelation 3:10

Those who keep the word by doing the spiritual works of God's Word will be protected during the *hour of temptation; the* travailing of mother earth.

And after these things I saw four angels standing on the four corners of the earth, holding the four winds of the earth, that the wind should not blow on the earth, nor on the sea, nor on any tree. And I saw another angel ascending from the east, having the seal of the living God: and he cried with a loud voice to the four angels, to whom it was given to hurt the earth and the sea, Saying, hurt not the earth, neither the sea, nor the trees, till we have sealed the servants of our God in their foreheads.
Revelation 7:1-3

The earth's tribulation, travailing, comes by way of earthly plagues, which are held up until the servants of God, the 144,000, are sealed. Those that do the works of judging the negative aspects of the twelve tribes of Israel become the servants of God, entering the wall of the new Jerusalem; an invisible wall of protection. When we allow the evil seeds of false beliefs to remain in our heart, we contribute to the negative and destructive energy coming upon the earth, adding to the intensity of the tribulation, the culmination of all of our collective evil. The evil or negative and destructive energy is increasing quickly because the world has entered the spiritual era of Jacob; man's spiritual evilness added to his physical evilness, bringing *"a time of trouble such as never was."*

For thus saith the Lord; We have heard a voice of trembling, of fear, and not of peace. Ask ye now, and see whether a man doth travail with child? wherefore do I see every man with his hands on his loins, as a woman in travail, and all faces are turned into paleness? Alas! for that day is great, so that none is like it: it is even the time of Jacob's trouble; but he shall be saved out of it. Jeremiah 30:5-8

And Jacob called unto his sons, and said, Gather yourselves together, that I may tell you that which shall befall you in the last days.
Genesis 49:1

Jacob refers to those that reclaim their spiritual birthright through a spiritual birth. It is the birth of spirit and truth (John 4:24), which takes place by overcoming the negative aspects of the twelve sons of Jacob.

And one of the elders answered, saying unto me, What are these that are arrayed in white robes? And whence came they? And I said unto him, Sir, thou knowest. And he said unto me, these are they which came out of great tribulation, and have washed their robes, and made them white in the blood of the Lamb. Therefore they are before the throne of God, and serve him day and night in his temple: and he that sitteth on the throne shall dwell among them. Revelation 7:13-15

The *great tribulation* is the birthing process. Those that come out of it by completing the process, have washed their robes of sinful flesh in the *blood of the Lamb*, symbolizing the *death of the Righteousness* that once lived in them, which they have atoned for through a spiritual death, giving birth to righteous truth from within their spiritual *throne* or *temple,* symbolizing the heart, where truth now reigns supreme.

And men were scorched with great heat, and blasphemed the name of God, which hath power over these plagues; and they repented not to give him glory. And the fifth angel poured out his vial upon the seat of the beast; and his kingdom was full of darkness; and they gnawed their tongues for pain, And blasphemed the God of heaven because of their pains and their sores, and repented not of their deeds. Revelation 16:9-11

Even the purifying plagues of earth will not bring those most deeply rooted in religion, *the seat of the beast*, to their knees. They will go down with the false gods that are the false beliefs they worship, dwelling in outer darkness, totally unaware of the negative and destructive energy that exists inside of them.

Then shall the cities of Judah and inhabitants of Jerusalem go, and cry unto the gods unto whom they offer incense: but they shall not save them at all in the time of their trouble. Jeremiah 11:12

The tribulation or time of trouble, coming in the form of physical and spiritual plagues, comes to move us out of spiritual *Sodom* and out of spiritual *Egypt;* out of *iniquity* or *sin*, and subsequently, out of physical and spiritual *bondage.*

And I will give power unto my two witnesses... And when they have finished their testimony, the beast that ascendeth out of the bottomless pit shall make war against them, and shall overcome them, and kill them. And their bodies shall lie in the street of the great city, which spiritually

*is called Sodom and Egypt, where also our Lord was crucified.
Revelation 11:3,7,8*

The *two witnesses,* spiritually, are *love and truth*. When we first entered this world, these two witnesses had power, ruling over our mind and heart. But in the process of time, that power was usurped through fear and lies, giving power to the *beast,* symbolizing the *false beliefs* that took possession of our heart. Those that use the challenge of tribulation as an opportunity to complete their transformation process, removing the flesh that is the beast, will become *"the last Adam... a quickening spirit."* And like Noah, they will enter an invisible ark of protection, entering the safety of the covenant God made with righteous Noah.

For in the time of trouble he shall hide me in his pavilion: in the secret of his tabernacle shall he hide me, he shall set me up upon a rock.
Psalms 27:5

All while the flood of evilness continues to rise upon the earth, engulfing the hearts of those that fight against seeing themselves. The purpose of tribulation is to get us to cry out from our heart, activating the process that will take us on a journey through our own mind and heart.

Chapter Ten
The Passover

The children of Israel kept the Passover as they were passing over from Egypt to the wilderness. They passed over from one place or state into another; from darkness into light, illustrated by the plague of darkness in Egypt. The Egyptians had three days of darkness, but the Israelites had light. What brings us into spiritual darkness is the absence of spiritual light; truth. There were three hours of darkness following the death of the light of the world, Jesus, as it is written, *"Now from the sixth hour there was darkness over all the land unto the ninth hour." Matthew 27:45.* The three hours or days of darkness, represent three thousand years of spiritual darkness. To understand what caused the death of God's word, the light of spiritual truth, bringing spiritual darkness to mankind, we must go to the story of Jonah, who spent three days and three nights in darkness, in the belly of the fish.

Now the word of the Lord came unto Jonah the son of Amittai, saying, Arise, go to Nineveh, that great city, and cry against it; for their wickedness is come up before me. But Jonah rose up to flee unto Tarshish from the presence of the Lord, and went down to Joppa; and he found a ship going to Tarshish: so he paid the fare thereof, and went down into it, to go with them unto Tarshish from the presence of the Lord. Jonah 1:1-3

The Lord has instructed Jonah to go to *Nineveh,* whose root meaning is *progeny, son; to resprout.* Nineveh is the capital of *Assyria,* meaning *to be successful, to go forward, to be honest, prosper.*

To reach this *son* state, we must cry against the spiritual wickedness that exists in our heart. The word of the Lord came to Jonah prior to his three days of darkness, in the belly of the *fish,* as Jesus came to the world prior to its three days of darkness, in the *age of Pisces.* We are in the third day of darkness; in the third-thousandth year of spiritual darkness. What caused the spiritual light of the world to be snuffed out can be seen in Jonah's decision to reject God's word, and go to *Tarshish,* meaning *a place on the Mediterranean; the epithet of a merchant vessel.* A merchant is one who buys and sells. Men have become spiritual merchants, buying and selling graven images of the spiritual kind in the spiritual temple (John 2:16).

And they set up Micah's graven image, which he made all the time that the house of God was in Shiloh. Judges 18:31

The word *Shiloh* means *an epithet of the Messiah.* Epithet is a term used to characterize the nature of a person or a thing. The nature of the Messiah is light. Jonah chose darkness.

Now the Lord had prepared a great fish to swallow up Jonah. And Jonah was in the belly of the fish three days and three nights.
Jonah 1:17

A *great fish* symbolizes a *great taxation,* which spiritually is to make a choice, which took place two thousand years ago in the age of *Pisces,* whose symbol is the *fish.* The people were being taxed to make a choice between the physical law and the spiritual word of God, between a physical kingdom and a spiritual kingdom, between bondage and freedom. Each age consists of a little over 2000 years (i.e., two days), the darkness caused by religious iniquity existing well into the age of *Aquarius,* whose symbol is the *water-bearer,* water having both a negative and positive connotation; iniquity and truth. This religious *graven image* will stand well into the thousand year reign of Christ, which has already begun. To pass over from the darkness of religious iniquity to the light of spiritual truth, will require us to hold a spiritual passover.

Holding the Spiritual Passover

And the Lord spake unto Moses and Aaron in the land of Egypt, saying, This month shall be unto you the beginning of months: it shall be the first month of the year unto you. Speak ye unto all the congregation of Israel, saying, In the tenth day of this month they shall take to them every man a lamb, according to the house of their fathers, a lamb for an house. Exodus 12:3

The *tenth day,* like the *tenth plague,* is about *death.* The word *tenth,* means *an accumulation, ten, to tithe, i.e. take or give a tenth.*

Will a man rob God? Yet ye have robbed me. But ye say, Wherein have we robbed thee? God's reply: *In tithes and offerings. Malachi 3:8*

Tithing is not about giving a tenth of your income to the Church. It's about gathering up and sacrificing what is destroying your physical and spiritual life. When one offers carnal tithes, omitting spiritual tithing, or sacrifice, one is breaking God's Commandment— *"Thou shalt not steal."* Offering carnal tithes or sacrifices is stealing from God because what God wants is spiritual; a right spirit and a repentant and purified heart. We are to sacrifice a spiritual *lamb,* symbolizing our *self-righteousness. A lamb for an house.* We are each a house, responsible for gathering up and sacrificing our own lamb of sin. The *lamb* that Israel gathered up was *according to their fathers,* the traditions of which are vain; of no value with respect to spiritual life.

Ye are of your father the devil, and the lusts of your father ye will do. He was a murderer from the beginning, and abode not in the truth, because there is no truth in him. When he speaketh a lie, he speaketh of his own: for he is a liar, and the father of it. John 8:44

The *devil* is the *lie,* a murderer of truth, a father that has sown the evil seeds of false beliefs into our heart, through which we sacrificed the *Lamb of God,* symbolizing *Righteous Truth,* breaking another Commandment— *"Thou shalt not kill,"* or more precisely, *"You are not to murder"* Exodus 20:13

Your lamb shall be without blemish, a male of the first year: ye shall take it out from the sheep, or from the goats: Exodus 12:5

The lamb we gather up and put on the altar is not without blemish. The scripture is prophetic; revealing what the people of Israel would do fifteen hundred years down the road. Instead of sacrificing their own lamb of sin, they sacrificed the Lamb of God, one *without blemish;* without sin. He was *a male of the first year,* taken out from the *sheep,* symbolizing the *Jews,* and from the *goats,* symbolizing the *Gentiles,* murdered in the first year; in 1 AD. Father Abraham illustrated this sacrifice of innocence two thousand years earlier when he put his son on the altar. We have all put the spiritual son of God on the spiritual altar of our heart, sacrificing the truth of our heart through false beliefs. Abraham's sacrifice also illustrated what should have taken place two thousand years ago, and what should be taking place now, at what is the start of the spiritual passover of the world, as Abraham ultimately sacrificed the *ram,* symbolizing *idolatry,* the worshipping of false images. It is our false religious and personal images or beliefs that we are to sacrifice, atoning for the death of truth that has taken place within us. Jesus, the spiritual Son of God the Father, died because of our sins, not in place of them, as religion teaches. Truth dies because of our iniquities, because of our sins (Isaiah 53:5).

Ye shall keep it up until the fourteenth day of the same month: and the whole assembly of the congregation of Israel shall kill it in the evening.
Exodus 12:6

The children of Israel were to *keep it up,* keep gathering up the lamb. But there is something more, referring to the actual Passover itself, which they were to keep observing until the *fourteenth day.* In God's cycle of time, the fourteenth day was two thousand years ago. Jesus came in the fifth day; in the beginning of the fifth thousandth year: $1+2+3+4+(5) = 15$. It was time to end carnal sacrificing, and commence with spiritual sacrificing. But they rejected the spiritual word of God, and *the congregation of Israel,* Jews and Gentiles alike, killed the Lamb of God on the *evening* of *the fourteenth day,* the days counted from evening to morning.

And they shall take the *blood and strike it on the two side posts and on the upper door post of the houses, wherein they shall eat it.*
Exodus 12:7

The *blood* symbolizes *death.* The *two side posts* symbolize the *two spiritual pillars* or witnesses of the heart. The *upper door post* is the head of the door, the *head* symbolizing *authority.* And what has had authority over man, and is to be put to death, is man's unholy spirit and unrighteous word. Through this spiritual sacrifice we make atonement for the death of God's spirit and word, illustrated two thousand years ago by the beheading of John the Baptist and the crucifixion of Jesus the Christ. We are to keep the spiritual passover, through which we restore the power of these two internal witnesses of the heart, giving power and authority to God's positive creative, and constructive creative energy in our life.

And they shall eat the flesh in that night, roast with fire, and unleavened bread; and with bitter herbs they shall eat it. Exodus 12:8

The *flesh* that is to be utterly consumed is our *false word.* The *flesh* they were to *eat* of two thousand years ago was *God's word.* They sacrificed the wrong flesh. The *night* symbolizes *darkness,* which the world entered literally upon the death of

Jesus, and spiritually upon the death of spiritual truth. It is in this night of spiritual darkness that man is to eat of the spiritual flesh or word of God. *"And the word was made flesh."* To *eat* means to *accept* into our heart, through obedience. The *fire* symbolizes the *spiritual judgment* that consumes our lamb of sin. The word *bread* means *to overcome.* The word *unleavened* means *without sin,* the spiritual state we reach by overcoming the false beliefs that make up our lamb of sin. The *bitter herbs* symbolize the *bitterness* associated with the death of truth. When we put the word of truth to death, we became confused, causing us to make wrong choices in our life, the negative consequences of which have caused us to become bitter. Jesus was given gall mixed with vinegar to drink upon his death, illustrating the bitterness that results from sacrificing the truth that wants to live in our heart.

Eat not of it raw, nor sodden at all with water, but roast with fire; his head with his legs, and with the purtenance thereof. Exodus 12:9

There are three ways we can go during the spiritual passover of the world. Three things we can do with the *flesh* of our lamb of self-righteousness. We can *eat of it raw,* which is to do nothing to correct our word of error. We can *sodden it with water,* which is to add even more iniquity. Or we can *roast it with fire,* which is to consume the flesh of our lamb of self-righteousness through a spiritual *fire; judgment* that consumes our word of error, restoring God's word of truth.

And ye shall let nothing of it remain until the morning: and that which remaineth of it until the morning ye shall burn with fire. Exodus 12:10

This sinful flesh is to be consumed out of our life, in this lifetime! Nothing of it is to remain by the *morning,* symbolizing the *resurrection.* That which remains will be consumed through a judgment in the afterlife; in the reality of God's kingdom. *"Let no man leave of it till the morning,"* Exodus

16:19. This was Moses' instruction to the children of Israel pertaining to the *manna*, symbolizing the *law of bondage or flesh*, which the children of Israel ate of, remaining under the bondage of the *carnal law*, for forty years. They spent the rest of their lives under a law that could not perfect them, having no power to consume this sinful flesh.

If therefore perfection were by the Levitical priesthood, (for under it the people received the law) what further need was there that another priest should rise after the order of Melchisedec, and not be called after the order of Aaron? Hebrews 7:11

Perfection requires the destruction of this flesh through the spiritual fire of a spiritual judgment— a spiritual holocaust.

And thus shall ye eat it; with your loins girded, and your shoes on your feet, and your staff in your hand; and ye shall eat it in haste: it is the Lord's passover. Exodus 12:11

He who takes part in this spiritual passover will be *girded* in righteousness, his spiritual lamb of self-righteousness consumed through the process. Having *shoes on your feet* symbolizes being *shod with the gospel* of truth. His *staff* symbolizes his *holy spirit*, which delivers the truth that consumes this invisible sinful flesh. We are to *eat it in haste*, get on with it, as the Lord's passover is already in progress.

There are four passovers; two physical, and two spiritual, coinciding. Our first physical passover takes place at birth, when we pass over from the darkness of the womb into the light. The next two are spiritual. When we pass over from spiritual darkness to levels of spiritual light or self-awareness, and when we pass over from the kingdom of heaven to the kingdom of God; from purifying our mind to purifying our heart. Our second physical passover takes place when we die.

Josiah holds the Greatest Passover

Josiah was eight years old when he began to reign, and he reigned in Jerusalem one and thirty years. And he did that which was right in the sight of the Lord, and walked in the ways of David his father, and declined neither to the right hand, or to the left. For in the eighth year of his reign, while he was yet young, he began to seek after the God of David his father: and in the twelfth year he began to purge Judah and Jerusalem from the high places, and the groves, and the carved images, and the molten images. And he brake down the altars of Baalim in his presence; and the images, that were high above them, he cut down; and the groves, and the carved images, he brake in pieces, and made dust of them, and strowed it upon the graves of them that had sacrificed unto them. And he burnt the bones of the priests upon their altars, and cleansed Judah and Jerusalem. 2 Chronicles 34:1-5

Josiah, meaning *founded of Jehovah,* was the *king of Judah,* symbolizing the *spirit of the Heart.* He was *eight years old* when he began to reign, *eight* meaning *a surplus above the "perfect seven,"* the word *seven* meaning *to be complete,* referring to the process that removes sinful flesh, perfecting the spirit of the heart. The removal of this invisible flesh is called circumcision, performed in the physical at eight days old (Genesis 17:12). It was in the eighth year of his reign that Josiah began *to seek after the God of David,* which is *to seek the God of the Heart;* David being a man after God's own Heart (1 Samuel 13:14). Or we might say, *seek the Kingdom of God.* In the *twelfth* year, the number *twelve* representing *judgment,* Josiah purges Judah and Jerusalem by destroying what constitutes the corruption of the temple. Josiah made *dust* of the false images, as we are to become *inactive* to our false beliefs through their destruction, no longer living to them through actions that support them. Judah and Jerusalem are purged, made clean through this temple purification process.

Judah was the tribe called out to bear *the name,* which is truth. *Jerusalem,* symbolizing *the mother,* serves to protect this truth.

Him that overcometh will I make a pillar in the temple of my God, and he shall go no more out: and I will write upon him the name of my God, and the name of the city of my God, which is new Jerusalem, which cometh down out of heaven from my God: and I will write upon him my new name. Revelation 3:12

We are to pass over from the old Jerusalem to the new Jerusalem by no longer protecting our unholy spirit and unrighteous word, passing over from the covenant of bondage to the covenant of freedom, and from false peace to true peace.

And the king commanded all the people, saying, Keep the passover unto the Lord your God, as it is written in the book of this covenant. Surely there was not holden such a passover from the days of the judges that judged Israel, nor in all the days of the kings of Israel, nor of the kings of Judah. 2 Kings 23:21, 22

It is the greatest passover ever held because it represents God's spiritual passover, held spiritually, as God intended. This spiritual passover could not take place in the days of the judges, or in the days of the kings of Israel and Judah, because they held to carnality. But now, in the spiritual era of Jacob, it will be held in the mind and heart of spiritual *disciples*; those who follow the spiritual teachings of Jesus, performing the spiritual works, through which their mind and heart is made pure.

My time is at hand; I will keep the passover at thy house with my disciples... And as they did eat, he said, Verily I say unto you, that one of you shall betray me. Matthew 26:18,21

Judas betrayed Jesus at passover two thousand years ago. Achan, of the tribe of Judah, took of the accursed thing at passover thirty-five hundred years ago (Joshua 5:10; 7:1). *Judas* is Greek for *Judah*. What betrays the truth is *iniquity*, which the *accursed thing* symbolizes.

Now this man (Judas) *purchased a field with the reward of iniquity... that field is called in their proper tongue, Aceldama, that is to say, The field of blood. Acts 1:18,19*

Iniquity is sin. *"And the wages of sin is death."* Romans 6:23. The *field* symbolizes the *world*, the *blood* symbolizing *death;* physical and spiritual death.

And the Jews' passover was at hand, and Jesus went up to Jerusalem, And found in the temple those that sold oxen and sheep and doves... And when he had made a scourge of small cords, he drove them out of the temple, and the sheep, and the oxen; and poured out the changers' money, and overthrew the tables; And he said unto them that sold doves, Take these things hence; make not my Father's house an house of merchandise. John 2:13-16

The spiritual passover is at hand. It is time to overturn the false images that we, as spiritual merchants, have sold to ourselves, setting them up in our spiritual temple, upon *"the fleshy tables of the heart."*

Instructions following the Passover

...and in the seventh day there shall be a holy convocation to you; no manner of work shall be done in them, save that which every one must eat, that only may be done of you. Exodus 12:16

The *seventh* day follows our six (metaphorical) days of (spiritual) works. It is through these works that we pass over from our old way of life into a new way of life, made possible through the creation of a new heaven and a new earth, symbolizing a new mind and a new heart. The *holy convocation* is a *holy ceremony*, a spiritual marriage, the conception of the *holy seed*, sown through the *holy spirit*. Once the holy seed of truth is conceived in the heart, the work is finished.

And you are to observe the feast of unleavened bread... In the first month, on the fourteenth day of the month at even, ye shall eat unleavened bread, until the one and twentieth day of the month at even.
Exodus 12:17,18

The time of conception is the *fourteenth*, when the holy seed of God was sown into the earth two thousand years ago. Man was to conceive of spiritual truth at that time, keeping the feast of unleavened bread by living the words of Jesus, through which he would overcome sin. Man was to continue working on overcoming his sin until the eve of the *one and twentieth day*, which is now: $1+2+3+4+5+6 = 21$. In the year 2000 we entered the seventh day, the next thousand years completing God's full cycle of time: $1+2+3+4+5+6+7 = 28$. And it may not be a thousand years, as it speaks of the days being shortened. If man had followed Jesus' instruction on purification from the beginning, he would have entered this seventh day holy, keeping God's Sabbath day holy.

As we leave the era of Isaac and enter the era of Jacob, we are given one last opportunity to take part in a spiritual passover. Jacob illustrates this passing over from bondage to freedom by entering the land of Laban, his father-in-law, where he goes into servitude to *Laban*, meaning *to be (or become) white*. He works seven years for Leah, seven years for Rachel, and six years for his wages, bringing him to the end of twenty (Genesis 31:41). The number seven pertains to the spiritual; to the spiritual works that purify the Mind and Heart, which Leah and Rachel represent. Jacob leaves his father-in-law, which represents coming out from under the law of bondage, the process for which is encoded in an event that took place following Jacob's exodus, when he wrestles with the man, which is to wrestle with our own mind and heart, *"until the breaking of the day;"* until we come into the light of their unholy inhabitants, which we must fight against in order to be free. This is our spiritual labor; spiritual works, through which we reclaim our spiritual birthright, separating ourselves from Esau. At the end of twenty-one, Jacob passes over into the land of *Shalem*, meaning *complete, perfect*, his works finished, found perfect before God (Revelation 3:2), the works of the six churches, completed, through which we are perfected.

As we leave the era of Isaac, we are being taxed, as they were two thousand years ago. It is a spiritual taxation, which is to make a choice at this spiritual passover. We choose Esau, forfeiting our spiritual birthright, by doing nothing, which is to *"eat of it raw,"* or by adding even more iniquity or sin, which is to *"sodden with water."* We choose Jacob by reclaiming our spiritual birthright through the spiritual works of a spiritual judgment that consumes our sin, which is to *"roast with fire."* Once our spiritual lamb of self-righteousness or sin is consumed, we are to keep the feast of unleavened bread. We are to eat no leaven; accept no sin in that spiritual womb called the heart, which must enter a pure state to conceive of God's holy seed of truth, as it is written, *"Behold, a virgin shall conceive, and bear a son, and shall call his name Immanuel,* meaning *with us is God.*

No manner of work was to be done in the seventh day. But man, possessed by the *"spirit of slumber* (Romans 11:8), has not been performing the spiritual works taught by Jesus two thousand years ago; in the beginning of the 5th day. If he had, he would be finished by now, entering this 7th day; God's day of rest, holy. It is time to hold the greatest passover ever by passing over from darkness to light; from lies to truth, from bondage to freedom, from within!

Then Moses called for all the elders of Israel, and said unto them, Draw out and take you a lamb according to your families, and kill the passover. Exodus 12:21

...It is the sacrifice of the Lord's passover, who passed over the houses of the children of Israel in Egypt, when he smote the Egyptians, and delivered our houses... Exodus 12:27

Chapter Eleven
The Two Kingdoms

In my Father's house are many mansions. The word *mansions* means *to stay (in a given place, state, relation, or expectancy)* revealing their spiritual element. These mansions exist in the *kingdom of heaven* and the *kingdom of God;* in the *realm of the mind* and the *realm of the Heart.* We choose the mansion in which we exist by choosing the state in which we wish our mind and heart to exist. We enter the kingdom of heaven by choosing to learn about the thoughts of our mind. It is our schoolroom, a place for learning about our self. Here we will ask questions pertaining to our life, eating of the spiritual *manna,* meaning *what? how? where?* and *why?* By eating of this spiritual *bread* from our spiritual heaven, we *overcome* that which is causing problems in our life.

Again, the kingdom of heaven is like unto a net, that was cast into the sea, and gathered every kind: Which, when it was full, they drew to shore, and sat down, and gathered the good into vessels, but cast the bad away. Matthew 13:47,48

The kingdom of heaven is like a net, which we are to cast into the deepest depths of our mind, retrieving all manner of thought, casting away the bad or negative and destructive thoughts through the process.

Woe unto them that call evil good, and good evil; that put darkness for light, and light for darkness... Isaiah 5:20

We have all called evil good, putting darkness for light by mistaking lies for truth, causing us to make wrong decisions throughout our life, which brought *woe*, meaning *misery*. We have pushed the negative and destructive energy of painful memories down into the darkness of the subconscious mind. It is time to bring that which is in darkness into the light, so the negative and destructive energy can be transformed into positive and constructive or creative energy.

Entering the Kingdom of Heaven

The people which sat in darkness saw great light; and to them which sat in the region and shadow of death light is sprung up. From that time Jesus began to preach, and to say, Repent: for the kingdom of heaven is at hand. Matthew 4:16,17

The *great light* is awareness with regard to the negative and destructive thoughts of our mind, some of which are hidden in the darkness of repression. The word *shadow* means *the darkness of error*. Error is sin, and the wages of sin is *death;* spiritual and physical death. The word *repent* means *to think differently*, taking place in the *kingdom of heaven*, symbolizing the *realm of the mind*. We enter the kingdom of heaven through a desire to change our life, activating a process that begins with changing our thoughts, the holy spirit bringing the negative and destructive thoughts or memories, hidden in the darkness of repression, into the light; into our awareness.

The land of Zabulon (Zebulun), and the land of Nephtalim (Naphtali) by the way of the sea, beyond Jordan, Galilee of the Gentiles.
Matthew 4:15

It is the *Gentiles* that come into the light. A spiritual Gentile is one that is open-minded; one that is willing to learn about oneself. The land of the Gentiles begins at *Zebulun* and ends at *Naphtali,* which has to do with us becoming aware of the destructive thoughts we have become inhabited with, and then becoming aware of the erroneous beliefs that generate them. When we experience this stage of the spiritual process, we have passed over from the kingdom of heaven to the kingdom of God.

For I say unto you, That except your righteousness shall exceed the righteousness of the scribes and Pharisees, ye shall in no case enter into the kingdom of heaven. Matthew 5:20.

Woe unto you, scribes and Pharisees, hypocrites! for ye make clean the outside of the cup and of the platter, but within they are full of extortion and excess. Thou blind Pharisee, cleanse first that which is within the cup and platter that the outside of them may be clean also.
Matthew 23:25,26

The *scribes and Pharisees* were the religious peoples of Jesus' day. The (self) *righteousness* of the hypocrite comes by making the outside look good. To exceed this phony external righteousness, we must clean the inside of the cup and the platter; the *cup* symbolizing the *mind,* the *platter* symbolizing the *heart,* purifying the thoughts of our mind and the emotions of our heart. We enter the kingdom of heaven through our desire to begin this life-changing purification process.

Another parable spoke he unto them; The kingdom of heaven is like unto leaven, which a woman took, and hid in three measures of meal, till the whole was leavened. Matthew 13:33

Leaven symbolizes *iniquity, error, sin.* If it is hid from us, we will add more sin, adding to the negative and destructive energy. *Leaven,* which causes the dough to swell or puff up, symbolizes *self-righteousness,* the result of accepting the *iniquity*; of mistaking the lies or our mind for truth.

The kingdom of heaven is likened unto a man which sowed good seed in his field: But while men slept, his enemy came and sowed tares among the wheat, and went his way. But when the blade was sprung up, and brought forth fruit, there appeared the tares also... The servants said unto him, Wilt thou then that we go and gather them up? But he said, Nay; lest while ye gather up the tares, ye root up also the wheat with them. Let both grow together until the harvest...: and in the time of harvest I will say to the reapers, Gather ye together first all the tares, and bind them in bundles to burn them: but gather the wheat into my barn. Matthew 13:24-30

The *good seed* was sowed in the earth two thousand years ago. So too was the evil seed of iniquity, sown *while men slept,* possessed by *"the spirit of slumber."* We have all eaten of the tree of knowledge of good and evil, and are now *in the time of harvest,* when we are to gather *all the tares,* consuming all the evil through the spiritual fire of a spiritual judgment, following Jesus' instruction for the "end of days" harvest.

Be glad then, ye children of Zion, and rejoice in the Lord your God: for he hath given you the former rain moderately, and he will cause to come down for you the rain, the former rain, and the latter rain in the first month. And the floors shall be full of wheat, and the fats shall overflow with wine and oil. Joel 2:23,24

The *rain* symbolizes the *outpouring of the spirit. Elijah,* symbolizing the *Spirit of God,* told Ahab there would be no rain, only according to his word. And there was no dew or rain, until the third year. We are in the beginning of the third year; the beginning of the third thousandth year since the good seed was sown in the earth. The rain or outpouring of the spirit is giving increase to whatever seed has been sown in the heart, be it good or evil. Elijah's return is spiritual; returning through the activation of the holy spirit; a whirlwind that stirs from within, separating the chaff from the wheat— the lies from the truth. This is our spiritual labor.

The harvest truly is plenteous, but the labourers are few… Matthew 9:37

We are the laborers. Not Jesus, as religion teaches. We will have to put in the work. Those that think they are born again and saved or already spirit and perfected before they have gone through the labor that brings them to that state, might want to think differently about that notion.

Before she travailed, she brought forth; before her pain came, she was delivered of a man child. Who hath heard such a thing? Who hath seen such things? Shall the earth be made to bring forth in one day…
Isaiah 66:7,8

We must labor to complete the process of spiritual birth or delivery, which means going through the *pain;* spiritual or emotional, pain. This process is not done *in one day.* Our heart is not changed in an instant; a false belief established through the deception or delusion of the mind, the route many unfortunately have chosen to take. It takes time for the *earth,* symbolizing the *heart,* to bring forth her fruit. So we need to get on with it. The time of the harvest is now!

The harvest is past, the summer is ended, and we are not saved.
Jeremiah 8:20

Salvation comes by replacing our word of error with God's word of truth, removing the wall of flesh formed inside of our physical flesh, leaving us pure spirit in essence, perfected through our spiritual labor.

At that same time came the disciples unto Jesus, saying, Who is the greatest in the kingdom of heaven? And Jesus called a little child unto him, and set him in the midst of them. And said, Verily I say unto you, Except ye be converted, and become as little children, ye shall not enter into the kingdom of heaven. Whosoever therefore shall humble himself as this little child, the same is the greatest in the kingdom of heaven.
Matthew 18:1-4

When we *humble* ourselves to the process, we enter the kingdom of heaven. The *Jordan,* meaning *a descender,* symbolizes this humble posture, the twelve stones placed in the Jordan symbolizing the spiritual judgment through which we *become as little children; pure* in thought, emotion, and action.

And I will give unto thee the keys of the kingdom of heaven: and whatsoever thou shalt bind on earth shall be bound in heaven: and whatsoever thou shalt loose on earth shall be loosed in heaven.
Matthew 16:19

We are given the keys to the *kingdom of heaven* through our desire to learn about ourselves. The *earth* is where seed is sown, the evil seed or false word being the cause of every negative and destructive thought we hold in our mind. If we are made free of the false word, we will be free of both the conscious and subconscious thought it generated, as it is written, *"For as he thinketh in his heart so he is"* (Proverbs 23:7). It's the heart that holds the key to freedom, possessing the power to release us from our spiritual and physical bondages.

Entering the Kingdom of God

...The kingdom of God cometh not with observation: Neither shall they say, Lo here!, or, lo there! for, behold, the kingdom of God is within you.
Luke 17:20,21

But seek ye first the kingdom of God, and his righteousness; and all these things shall be added unto you. Matthew 6:33

The *kingdom of God* symbolizes the *realm of the Heart.* We enter it by seeking the truth of the heart. If we only seek the righteousness of truth at the mind level, we will retain that which is keeping us from receiving what our heart truly desires.

Ye lust, and have not: ye kill, and desire to have, and cannot obtain... purify your hearts, ye double minded. James 4:1,8

If we purify our mind, but not our heart, we are *double minded* because the heart, dwelling of the subconscious mind, will hold one thought, while the conscious mind holds another. The mind becomes an enemy of the heart, hiding its true feelings and condition. We must seek the kingdom of God, seeking to *purify our hearts.*

In those days came John the Baptist, preaching in the wilderness of Judaea, And saying, Repent ye: for the kingdom of heaven is at hand.
Matthew 3:1,2

John the Baptist, who embodied the Spirit of God, preceded Jesus. John preached *repentance,* meaning *to think differently,* the *spirit* influencing the mind, serving to change the way we think, the precursor to entering the kingdom of God.

Then was Jesus led up of the spirit into the wilderness to be tempted of the devil. And when he had fasted forty days and forty nights, he was afterward an hungered. Matthew 4:1,2

Jesus is led by the spirit into the *wilderness,* symbolizing the *mind.* For *forty* days he performs a mind discipline, not accepting any untruthful thoughts into his mind, which is spiritual fasting. The children of Israel also spent time in the wilderness— *forty* years. But unlike Moses, they never ascended the mount; they never sought to purify their hearts. They remained under the mind-body discipline of the Law for the rest of their lives, never entering the Promised Land; never entering the kingdom of God.

Then came to him the disciples of John, saying, Why do we and the Pharisees fast oft, but thy disciples fast not? Matthew 9:14

And they said unto him, Why do the disciples of John fast often, and make prayers, and likewise the disciples of the Pharisees; but thine eat and drink? Luke 5:33

The disciples of John and *the Pharisees* practiced a mind-body discipline, which was to end at the death of John the Baptist, as the Law was to end at the death of Moses. John instructed his own disciples to stop following him, and follow Jesus, saying to his disciples, *"He must increase, but I must decrease."* The Spirit was now resting upon Jesus, becoming one with the word, the spirit working in conjunction with the works of the word, evoking a more powerful heart discipline.

And John bare record, saying, I saw the Spirit descending from heaven like a dove, and it abode upon him. John 1:32

The *works* of *repentance* was over, *dead,* symbolized by the beheading of John. It was time to move past ephemeral mind-body disciplines and into a lasting heart discipline; moving beyond the kingdom of heaven and into the kingdom of God, where we do the works that purify our heart.

...let us go on into perfection; not laying again the foundation of repentance from dead works, and of faith toward God, Of the doctrine of baptisms, and of laying on of hands, and resurrection of the dead, and of eternal judgment. Hebrews 6:1,2

John preached repentance, the spirit working through the mind, influencing our thoughts, causing us to think differently. The miracles Jesus performed were also of the spirit, healing body and mind. But Jesus spoke of greater works (John 14:12), taking place in the *kingdom of God* for the greater purpose of healing the heart, the deepest level of the soul, causing us to feel and believe differently. Jesus said, *though ye believe not me, <u>believe the works</u>"* (John 10:38).

For I say unto you, Among those that are born of women there is no greater prophet than John the Baptist: but he that is least in the kingdom of God is greater than he. Luke 7:28

Faith toward God is of the kingdom of heaven or realm of the mind, referring to the beginning of faith, where we see the things we hope for through our mind's eye. The *end of faith* is of the kingdom of God, where we do the works that makes what we hope for a reality.

Now faith is the substance of things hoped for, the evidence of things not yet seen. Hebrews 11:1

In the definition of *faith* we find the beginning of faith and the end of faith— visualization and actualization. What causes the things we hope for to become a reality, are the greater works Jesus spoke of. There are works of the spirit performed in the mind, in the kingdom of heaven. And there are works of the spirit performed in the heart, in the kingdom of God, the outpouring of the spirit in our mind and heart symbolized by the *former rain* and the *later rain*. (Jeremiah 5:24), through which we bring good fruit unto God.

If a brother or sister be naked, and destitute of daily food, And one of you say unto them, Depart in peace, be ye warmed and filled; notwithstanding ye give them not those things which are needful to the body; what doth it profit? Even so faith, if it hath not works, is dead, being alone. James 2:15-17

Helping someone on a physical level is a work of the Law. It can also be seen as a work of the Spirit with respect to the love and compassion we are showing towards them. While these acts of kindness make us feel good in the moment, the salvation of our soul is received through the deeper works of the spirit, which combined with the works of the word, heal the emotions of our heart— the *christ* healing power of the heart at work!

Receiving the end of your faith, even the salvation of your souls. Of which salvation the prophets have enquired and searched diligently...
1 Peter 1:9,10

John the Baptist embodied the spirit, advocating works associated with the mind and body (e.g., repentance, ritualistic baths, dietary laws, etc.). Jesus the Christ embodied the word, bringing our attention to the heart, moving beyond purification of the mind and body and into purification of the heart; moving beyond the kingdom of heaven and into the kingdom of God. There are *seven* impurities of the heart, which can only be eliminated through the spiritual works of the word, through which we receive *the salvation of our souls.*

For out of the heart proceed evil thoughts, murders, adulteries, fornications, thefts, false witness, blasphemies: These are the things which defile a man... Matthew 15:19,20

When he speaketh fair, believe him not, for there are seven abominations in his heart. Proverbs 26:25

Be watchful, and strengthen (be strong about) *the things which remain, that are ready to die: for I have not found thy works perfect before God. Revelation 3:2*

The word *seven* and *perfect* share the same meaning, *to be complete.* What makes us complete or perfect, is the word of God, which we receive by doing the works (John 10:35-38). It is through these spiritual works that we receive the salvation of our soul, our faith complete, perfected.

When the unclean spirit is gone out of a man, he walketh through dry places, seeking rest, and findeth none. Then he said, I will return into my house from whence I came out; and when he is come, he findeth it empty, swept, and garnished. Then goeth he, and taketh seven other spirits more wicked than himself, and they enter in and dwell there: and the last state of that man is worse than the first. Even so shall it be also unto this wicked generation. Matthew 12:43-45

Man has done a good job of purifying his thoughts, but he has yet to purify his heart. His works are not yet made perfect; not yet complete, so he finds no rest. He must enter the *kingdom of God,* where the enemy dwells.

If I cast out devils by the Spirit of God, then the kingdom of God is come unto you. Matthew 12:28

Now when Jesus was risen early the first day of the week, he appeared first to Mary Magdalene, out of whom he cast seven devils. Mark 16:9

For he said unto him, Come out of the man, thou unclean spirit. And he asked him, What is thy name? And he answered, saying, My name is Legion; for we are many. Mark 5:8,9

When you become aware of the false beliefs that inhabit your heart, *the kingdom of God is come unto you;* you have entered the kingdom of God. You have placed your feet on holy ground, where you are to fight a holy war, driving the unholy inhabitants out of your spiritual promised land, as the children of Israel were to drive the seven inhabitants out of the literal Promised Land.

The time is fulfilled, and the kingdom of God is at hand: repent, and believe the gospel. Mark 1:15

To *believe the gospel* is to *obey the works of the word,* through which we overcome *the works of the flesh.*

Now the works of the flesh are manifest, which are these; Adultery, fornication, uncleanness, lasciviousness, idolatry, witchcraft, hatred, variance, emulations, wrath, strife, seditions, heresies, envyings, murders, drunkenness, revellings, and such like: of the which I tell you before, as I have also told you in time past, that they which do such things shall not inherit the kingdom of God. Galatians 5:19-21

The *works of the flesh* refer not only to the physical acts committed by our external flesh, but more importantly, to the spiritual acts committed because of our internal flesh. If our heart is made pure, our thoughts and actions become pure. We inherit the kingdom of God through the purification of our heart, entering a pure spiritual state in which none of these works of the flesh could, or would, ever take place.

Verily, verily, I say unto thee, Except a man be born of water and of the Spirit, he cannot enter into the kingdom of God. That which is born of flesh is flesh; and that which is born of the Spirit is spirit. John 3:5,6

We were *born of water,* separated from a womb of water, at birth, being *born of flesh,* separated from our mother's flesh body. We are *born of water* through spiritual baptism, which is to be drawn up out of the waste in our life, separated, through truth, from the sinful flesh formed by our word of error, through which we become spirit in essence, the precursor to being *born of the Spirit.*

Marvel not that I said unto thee, Ye must be born again. The wind bloweth where it listeth, and thou hearest the sound thereof, but canst not tell whence it cometh, and whither it goeth: so is every one that is born of the Spirit. John 3:7,8

Jesus uses the *wind,* symbolizing *spirit,* to reveal the nature of spirit. The wind blows. You can hear the sound of it, but you can't tell from which direction it came, or in which direction it went, a characteristic of someone who is born of the spirit or born again, *"that which is born of the Spirit is spirit."* You can't see spirit. To be born spirit, our mother must be of spirit, which only happens when all of our internal sinful flesh has been removed. Then, when our external sinful flesh is removed upon our death, we will be born of the spirit upon resurrection, born free. If our internal flesh still remains upon our death, our mother is of flesh, and we will be born flesh, *"that which is born of the flesh is flesh,"* born in bondage, in a type of spiritual flesh that will limit us in the afterlife, as our invisible sinful flesh limited us in this life.

But he who was born of the bondwoman was born after the flesh; but he of the freewoman was by promise…for the son of the bondwoman shall not be heir with the son of the freewoman. Galatians 4:23, 30

The *promise* is truth, the builder of spirit. The holy spirit, if not resisted, brings the light of the truth that makes us free, the *"spirit of truth"* ((John 16:13) leading us into all [the] truth, removing the spiritual darkness formed by our word of false beliefs. The mansions in God's kingdom are levels of light, degrees of truth. With each false belief we expose and replace with truth, we remove a layer of flesh, making us more of truth, and therefore more of spirit (Jeremiah 4:4).

For the KINGDOM of GOD is not Food and Drink; but Righteousness, and Peace, and Joy in a holy Spirit. Romans 14:17

And he said, Whereunto shall we liken the *kingdom of God? or with what comparison shall we compare it? It is like a grain of mustard seed, which when sown in the earth, is less than all the seeds that be in the earth: But when it is sown, it groweth, and becometh greater than all herbs, and shooteth out great branches; so that the fowls of the air may lodge under the shadow of it. Mark 4:30-32*

The *kingdom of God* is the *realm of the Heart,* where seeds, good and evil, have been sown. These seeds grow and become great. What might have seemed like a small thing upon conception has grown into something quite large, having a huge impact on our life, without us even realizing it. The good seeds bring peace and joy, but the evil seeds bring pain and sorrow. When we remove all the evil seeds by removing all the false beliefs that occupy our heart, we will have completed our works in the kingdom of God, completing our six (metaphorical) days of (spiritual) works. A day is twenty four hours, 6 days formulating to *6 x 24*, which equals *144*, the measure of the wall of Jerusalem.

And he measured the wall thereof, an hundred and forty and four cubits, according to the measure of a man... Revelation 21:17

Our six days of spiritual works in the kingdom of heaven and the kingdom of God is the creation of our new spiritual heaven and earth; the creation of our new mind and heart. Completing our six days of spiritual works equates to judging the twelve tribes of Israel (Matthew 19:28), the number twelve representing judgment. Judging the twelve tribes of Israel formulates to *12x12,* which equals *144*, through which we *measure* up to God's standard, entering the holy city, *new Jerusalem*, entering *a new peaceful state* through the creation of a new mind and a new heart (Revelation 21:1-4).

Him that overcometh will I make a pillar in the temple of my God, and he shall go no more out: and I will write upon him the name of my God, and the name of the city of my God, which is new Jerusalem... Revelation 3:12

Those who complete the spiritual works or judgment, enter the thousand-year reign of Christ, which when added to 144 brings them to a measure of *an hundred and forty and four thousand,* the measure of the bride ..." *Come hither, I will show thee the bride, the Lamb's wife"* (Revelation 21:9).

And I heard the number of them which were sealed: and there were sealed an hundred and forty and four thousand of all the tribes of the children of Israel. Revelation 7:4

Note: There is no tribe of Dan listed among the 144,000 that were sealed. This is because Dan represents judgment, and there will be no judgment upon the 144,000 because they have already judged themselves.

And the city had no need of the sun, neither of the moon, to shine in it: for the glory of God did lighten it, and the Lamb is the light thereof. And the nations of them which are saved shall walk in the light of it: and the kings of the earth do bring their glory and honour into it. And the gates of it shall not be shut at all by day: for there shall be no night there... And there shall in no wise enter into it any thing that defileth, neither whatsoever worketh abomination, or maketh a lie: but they which are written in the Lamb's book of life. Revelation 21:23-27

A description of the kingdom of God, the word *city* meaning *to have your eyes opened*. And what we are to have our eyes opened to, is ourselves, seeing the error that exists in us in the form of false perceptions and beliefs, and then overcoming them. The light of the city comes neither from the sun or the moon, but from the *Lamb* of God, symbolizing *Righteous Truth*. The *sun* symbolizes our *father*, and the *moon* symbolizes our *mother* (Genesis 37:9,10), their false perceptions, which we accepted as truth, darkened (Joel 3:15), eclipsed by the light of truth. The *nations of them which are saved* are spiritual nations. Judging the negative aspects of these nations or tribes is the process of salvation, through which we *walk in the light* of the city. The *kings of the earth* symbolize the *spirits of the heart*. When the negative and destructive spirits of the heart give way to positive and constructive spirits, it brings *a new state of being*, bringing glory and honor to the holy city, *new Jerusalem*. There is *no night* in the city because all that has been hidden in the darkness of repression, suppression, delusion, or denial, has been brought to light. There is nothing that *defileth* or worketh *abomination* because the heart has been purified.

With each false belief we overcome, we ascend into a greater degree of light, which being truth, contains a greater degree of spirit. If we become all truth by removing all falsehood, we ascend into the pure white light of the city, being pure spirit, having eternal life.

And he shewed me a pure river of water of life, clear as crystal, proceeding out of the throne of God and of the Lamb. In the midst of the street of it, on either side of the river, was there the tree of life, which bare twelve manner of fruit, and yielded her fruit every month: and the leaves of the tree were for the healing of the nations... and whosoever will, let him take of the water of life freely. Revelation 22:1,2,17

The *throne of God* is the kingdom of God. All life proceeds from the *throne,* symbolizing the *heart,* our quality of life determined by the condition of our heart; by our emotional state. We are each a *tree of life,* the *twelve manner of fruit* symbolizing the *spiritual judgment that yields the fruits of the spirit,* within. The word *leaves* means *tribe, to germinate, to spring up,* each tribe of Israel being an aspect of the internal healing process, which is the *healing of the nations;* the process of transforming the negative spirits or energies of the twelve tribes into positive spirits or energies. The *water of life* is God's *word of truth.* We *take of* it by obeying the spiritual works contained in God's Word.

God's kingdom, which consists of the kingdom of heaven and the kingdom of God, is within and without. Whatever our spiritual (mental and emotional) condition upon our death in this life will be our spiritual condition in the afterlife, determining whether we enter the kingdom of heaven or the kingdom of God upon resurrection.

Vision of the Kingdom
(as seen by the man of God on 7-7-77)

It is made up of 7 levels, the kingdom being the 8th, at the top. The land at the top is very flat—7 rings around the mount. As you go up, each one is smaller and higher than the last. The city is the smallest, which rests on the flat land at the very top (Benjamin's inheritance was the smallest, but the richest). The light from the kingdom only shines from the top to the bottom of the mount. It doesn't reach the foothills or plains or outer darkness. To reach the top of the mount you must go to the one higher than you are at, then one at that mount will take the message to the next higher mount, and so on. They cannot leave their mount, only to the outer border. Execution is outer darkness. The next worse judgment is just outside the plains.

The new Jerusalem will come down and set itself on the very top of the mount. All life comes from the kingdom—all healing power, all foods, and all drinks. The river flows down the mount out of the kingdom. The kingdom itself is not round, it is built in the shape of an altar and it's illuminated, it glows. The further out you go from the center of the kingdom (which is east), the further south you go. There are only three points of the compass, which go out from the kingdom. The kingdom being east (out of the east comes light), south—parched (Judah), north—smoke (from the foot of the mount out), and west—straight down. Each ring represents a city, and each ring will be the torment of the inner ring (the outer ring the torment of the inner ring). Edom is the last place before the bottomless pit. Outer darkness is entirely black. The smoke of their torment will rise up forever and ever. It will never cease. The smoke rises up, drifting over the flat lands, covering it. It never reaches over the mount, which is always clearly visible. Out of the north comes trouble, like smoke (torment, punishment). The lake of fire is entirely around the outer edge. Jerusalem is Joseph and Benjamin. People that come out of the tribulation are right outside Joseph.

Simeon and Levi are under the smoke. The river circles the foot of the mount. The people are like cattle coming and drinking at the river that flows out of the kingdom. The two and three quarter million that came out of Egypt will be around the foot of the mount. There's a ring between carnal Israel and the foot of the mount. Just outside of the river is Moses. He can see across the river (he saw the Promised Land, it's the promise).

Moses himself will be in the kingdom, but Moses, representing the law, are those that have lived under the law. The river is low down. Nobody outside the river can cross the river. This is Reuben, Gad, and Manasseh, who received their inheritance before they crossed the Jordan River. The river is outside the foothills. In the foothills is where Israel is.

The mount will be called Jacob. On the mount are all the commandments and statutes, and those that have kept the commandments and statutes of God. The tablets of stone (the law) were carried down the mount. I see it like a cloud, rolling down the mount. When it spreads out over the foothills, it's like a fog that settles over the people. I keep hearing "break in pieces." The mount shaking is the wrath of God. The law becomes stones that are shattered to pieces when the mount shakes, (which is the wrath of God) scattering over the people. The mount will shake under the city. The city is not connected to the mount. The city is sitting on twelve columns. The separation on the mount is the separation between carnal and spiritual. They'll never see the glory of the city.

There will be people that won't plead guilty or innocent. They won't admit they have done anything wrong, and because of their guilt of knowing they have done wrong, they will neither admit they have done anything good. These people are mutes.

Chapter Twelve
The Two Resurrections

There are two resurrections, corresponding with the two kingdoms. The difference is in the degree of death that has taken place. Those, in whom all sinful flesh has died, take part in the first resurrection.

I know thy works, that thou has a name that thou livest, and art dead. Be watchful, and strengthen (be strong about) *the things which remain, that are ready to die: for I have not found thy works perfect ...*
Revelation 3:1,2

The word of God was made flesh. When that flesh, being without sin, died, there was a resurrection, an illustration of the first resurrection. Our word of error is also made flesh, a sinful flesh formed inside of our physical flesh, the wages of which is death, the second resurrection associated with *"the second death";* the death of the *the things that remain;* the false beliefs that formed this sinful flesh.

Behold, I was shapen in iniquity; and in sin did my mother conceive me. Behold thou desirest truth in the inward parts... Psalms 51:5,6

We were shaped by false perceptions and beliefs; in iniquity, and in sin. To purify our *inward parts,* symbolizing our mind and heart, requires truth, which takes away sin, removing the internal layers of sinful flesh formed by the false perceptions of our mind and the false beliefs of our heart. Our external layer of sinful flesh is removed from our soul upon our physical death.

The First Resurrection

And I saw thrones, and they that sat upon them, and judgment was given unto them: and I saw the souls of them that were beheaded for the witness of Jesus, and for the word of God, and which had not worshipped the beast, neither his image, neither had received his mark upon their foreheads, or in their hands; and they lived with Christ a thousand years. But the rest of the dead lived not again until the thousand years were finished. This is the first resurrection. Revelation 20:4,5

The *thrones* represent *seats of judgment* and *they that sat upon them* are those that have gone through this righteous spiritual judgment, cast into a spiritual lake of fire, through which the spiritual beast of their heart was consumed.

For if we would judge ourselves, we should not be judged.
1 Corinthians 11:31

And as it is appointed unto men once to die, but after this the judgment.
Hebrews 9:27

One physical death, after which comes the judgment. But if we judge ourselves, we die a spiritual death. We will still die a physical death, but it will not be followed by the judgment.

And Jesus said unto them, Verily, verily I say unto you, That ye which have followed me, in the regeneration when the Son of man shall sit in the throne of his glory, ye also shall sit upon twelve thrones, judging the twelve tribes of Israel. Matthew 19:28

We sit upon twelve metaphorical thrones as we judge (overcome) the negative aspects of the twelve tribes of Israel, which is the *regeneration;* the restoration of truth, the *throne* symbolizing the *heart.* The Son sits in the throne of his glory when truth rules our heart, which is the outcome of this spiritual judgment. We will still die a physical death because the physical body is sin, and the wages of sin is death, the consequence of accepting the error in the garden. But we will not be subject to *the second death* if we die to all of our sin through the resurrection of truth, having taken *part in the first resurrection* while on earth.

Blessed and holy is he that hath part in the first resurrection: on such the second death hath no power, but they shall be priests of God and of Christ, and shall reign with him a thousand years. Revelation 20:6

We are made *holy* through the purification of our heart. We become *priests of God and of Christ* by offering the spiritual *sacrifices of God* that purify our heart. We are *of Christ* when our heart is ruled by God's holy spirit and word; love and truth, whereby we reign with Christ. The *thousand years* is not about a literal period of time. It refers to the seventh day, in which this purification of the heart is to take place, which is now!

Create in me a clean heart, O God; and renew a right spirit within me. Cast me not away from thy presence; and take not thy holy spirit from me. Restore unto me the joy of thy salvation; and uphold me with thy free spirit. Then will I teach transgressors thy ways; and sinners shall be converted unto thee. Psalms 51:10-13

The sacrifices of God are a broken spirit: a broken and a contrite heart, O God, thou wilt not despise. Psalms 51:17

The *spirit* that is broken is our own spirit; the spirit of the flesh that has been formed by our word of error. *"Blessed are the poor in spirit: for theirs is the kingdom of heaven,"* the kingdom of heaven symbolizing the realm of the mind, which we inherit by overcoming the unholy spirit of our mind, which gives power to the lies of our mind. The word *contrite* means *to collapse (physically or mentally), break (in pieces), crush, destroy,* describing the emotional process called surrendering, through which we relinquish the power or control of our mind, giving power to the holy spirit of our heart.

O stiffnecked and uncircumcised in HEART and EARS! you always fight against the HOLY SPIRIT; as your FATHERS did you do also. Acts 7:51 (Greek Diaglott)

When we stop resisting the HOLY SPIRIT of our heart, it begins to influence the thoughts of our mind, exposing what is in the heart, bringing to light our word of error, exposing every false belief we've accepted into our heart. This false word makes up the flesh that covers the heart. With each false belief we remove, we remove a layer of flesh, which is circumcision of the heart. The more of truth we become, the more of spirit we become, our internal flesh moving through degrees of density, becoming lighter and lighter, which is the process of spiritual ascension. The third dimension is carnal, the fourth, transitional, and the fifth, spiritual.

Note: Most who have crossed over exist in one of the many levels that make up the kingdom of heaven, where they are learning and growing. They exist in what we might call a parallel universe, running parallel with us here on earth, having the same opportunity to ascend into the kingdom of God through the spiritual works that purify the heart.

The body we receive upon resurrection is determined by the degree of internal or spiritual flesh formed by our word of error. Our word is our seed, *to every seed his own body.* If our word is pure truth, we come forth as pure spirit, able to take on a body, glorified or physical, at will, which Jesus illustrated after his resurrection.

But some man will say, How are the dead raised up? and with what body do they come? ...that which thou sowest is not quickened, except it die: And that which thou sowest, thou sowest not the body that shall be, but bare grain, it may chance of wheat, or of some other grain: But God giveth it a body as it hath pleased him, and to every seed his own body. All flesh is not the same flesh... There are also celestial bodies, and bodies terrestrial: but the glory of the celestial is one, and the glory of the terrestrial is another. 1 Corinthians 15:35-40

The Second Resurrection

And when the thousand years are expired, Satan shall be loosed out of his prison. Revelation 20:7

This is the beginning of the second resurrection, which has already begun, in type. *Satan,* that old devil, the serpent, symbolizing *man's iniquity,* has been loosed from prison, no longer bound, running rampant. These are perilous times for those without understanding (Daniel 12:10), without the light of truth, the spiritual wedding garment that keeps us from dwelling in outer darkness, (Matthew 22:12,13).

Then, if any man shall say unto you, Lo, here is Christ, or there; believe it not. For there shall arise false Christs, and false prophets, and shall shew great signs and wonders; insomuch that, if it were possible, they shall deceive the very elect. Matthew 24:23,24

Religious iniquity has no bounds, carnal interpretations continuing to distract and deceive the people, many of whom are still looking for a physical return of Christ, for a show of great signs and wonders, or for a physical rapture that will take them out before the tribulation begins.

And I saw three unclean spirits like frogs come out of the mouth of the dragon, and out of the mouth of the beast, and out of the mouth of the false prophet. For they are the spirits of devils, working miracles, which go forth unto the kings of the earth and of the whole world, to gather them to the battle of that great day of God almighty. Revelation. 16:13,14

The *three unclean spirits like frogs* symbolize the *three evil spirits* of religion. The *mouth of the dragon* issues forth the promise of a fiery judgment upon those that do not accept the religious iniquity spewing forth from the *mouth of the beast,* the beast being the false religious belief. The *mouth of the false prophet* speaks lies, assigning carnal interpretations to the spiritual

Word of God. These modern day false prophets instill fear through their lies, and they do it with a heart of anger, seeking to control their followers through their oppressive and soul-destroying beliefs.

And they shall go out to deceive the nations which are in the four quarters of the earth, Gog and Magog, to gather them to battle: the number of whom is as the sand of the sea. Revelation 20:8

During this time, the tribulation of physical plagues will continue to increase upon the earth, causing those that refused to give up the beastly religious image to become more and more angry when they realize there's no Jesus coming in the clouds. They will rise up against the seed royal; against those reigning with Christ, crying, *"Treason, Treason,"* proclaiming that God has deceived them (2 Kings, Chapter 11).

Gog is a symbolic name for some future antichrist.
Magog is a foreign nation, i.e (fig.) an antichristian party.

Those that continue to buy into the beastly religious image are of the religious antichristian party, *anti,* meaning *against*. They are against christ because they fight against the spirit that would bring them a spiritual understanding of God's Word. By completing the spiritual works of the Word, they would resurrect *christ* from within. In resurrecting God's *spirit and word* from within, they would no longer be *anti christ*.

And they went up on the breadth of the earth, and compassed the camp of the saints about, and the beloved city: and fire came down from God out of heaven, and devoured them. Revelation 20:9

The spiritual Word of God will never be destroyed again!

And the devil that deceived them was cast into the lake of fire and brimstone, where the beast and the false prophet are, and shall be tormented day and night for ever and ever. Revelation 20:10

The *devil that deceived them* is the *iniquity that deceived them,* being one with the *beast;* the *beastly religious image* or *belief.* It is the false religious belief that makes them the *false prophet,* prophesying lies to themselves, and oftentimes, to others. If they do not destroy this beast and his image through judgment, they will remain bound by it, tormented by the deception of it all in the afterlife. This is hell, which has separated them from any degree of spiritual life, or light, a spiritual state called *"outer darkness."* Those that refuse to give up the beastly image, even after the plagues of the earth have come to reprove them, will know that they missed the boat, a knowledge that will torment them. This is the beginning of the second resurrection.

And I saw a great white throne, and him that sat on it, from whose face the earth and heaven fled away; and there was found no place for them.
Revelation 20:11

The *great white throne* symbolizes *God's righteous judgment,* from which the *earth and heaven,* symbolizing the *heart and mind,* has fled. There is *no place* found in God's kingdom for those that run from this spiritual judgment because it is within God's kingdom that the judgment of the mind and heart, takes place. To enter God's kingdom in the afterlife, we must first enter it in this life, entering our own mind and heart, where we judge (overcome) our false perceptions and beliefs. There is a window of opportunity in which to make this judgment on earth. When that window closes, the stage is set for the final act; the reality of God's Kingdom.

And I saw the dead, small and great, stand before God; and the books were opened, which is the book of life: and the dead were judged out of those things which were written in the books, according to their works.
Revelation 20:12

Resurrection is of the *dead*. Those of the first resurrection have experienced a spiritual death through a spiritual judgment, in this life. Those of the second resurrection are given an opportunity to experience *"the second death,"* in the afterlife. The *small and great* has nothing to do with earthly eminence. It has to do with spiritual eminence, which is measured by the amount of spiritual works accomplished on this side. The *books* symbolize the *lives* of every individual, which are opened up to us upon resurrection.

Note: Those having the ability to communicate with those on the other side, find no indication of any kind of external judgment. This is because, like us, they have an opportunity to go through a life review process, judging themselves. There is a window of opportunity for executing this internal judgment. When it closes, an external judgment will begin on earth, as well as in heaven; in the spiritual realm.

If there is such a thing as an opportunity to return to the earth school to learn, as some believe, that too will close. We are in the spiritual era of Jacob, in which man is given every opportunity, and all the information he needs to complete this spiritual judgment. Once that spiritual knowledge is made known, the earth school is no longer necessary. Wherever we process to during this final era determines where we end up in the reality of God's kingdom, as our works follow us into the spiritual realm. We may come forth in the city as pure spirit or as glorified beings; a state that allows us to partake of the greater spiritual rewards. Or we may come forth in the kingdom of heaven, where we will continue to learn about ourselves, growing in spirit. God's kingdom is light; levels of light, equal to the degrees of truth or understanding we have about ourselves. But if we continue to resist the holy spirit, which brings us into the spiritual light of understanding, we will find ourselves in outer darkness. Once the reality of the kingdom of heaven is set in place, those entering it will remain at the level they reached while on earth. They will still be able to progress, but will be limited by the realm of energy or vibration in which they existed upon their resurrection. The more negative and destructive energy and error we hold on to here on earth, the greater our limitations will be on earth, and in heaven; in the reality of God's kingdom.

And the sea gave up the dead which were in it; and death and hell delivered up the dead which were in them: and they were judged every man according to their works. Revelation 20:13

This will be played out on earth in a type of second resurrection. The *sea* symbolizes the *thoughts* and *memories* hidden in the depths of the mind; in the darkness of repression and denial. The sea gives up the dead when these negative and destructive thoughts and memories, which equate to *death*, are brought into the light, which is life. *Hell* is the mental and emotional state caused by these repressed thoughts and suppressed emotions. The *dead* are the spiritually dead; those that have not yet judged (overcome) these destructive thoughts and painful emotions, through which they would obtain spiritual life.

And death and hell were cast into the lake of fire. This is the second death. Revelation 20:14

If we live in *death and hell* on this side, we will live in death and hell on the other side. Those existing in this state will be cast into the *lake of fire*, symbolizing the *spiritual judgment* that brings them into a new state, where there is no more sea, no more pain, and no more death (Revelation 21:1-4). This spiritual judgment is *the second death*.

And whosoever was not found written in the book of life was cast into the lake of fire. Revelation 20:15

If we are living a life that is no life, living in a mental and emotional hell, we are spiritually dead in the bad sense, our name not written in *the book of life*. But we can gain spiritual life through God's spiritual judgment, which results in a spiritual death in the good sense. This is *the second death*.

But the fearful, and unbelieving, and the abominable, and murderers, and whoremongers, and sorcerers, and idolaters, and all liars, shall have their part in the lake which burneth with fire and brimstone: which is the second death. Revelation 21:8

The word *brimstone* goes to the Greek word *theos,* meaning *godlike*. It is through the *fire* of this spiritual judgment that we replace fear with love and lies with truth, restoring God's spirit and word from within, becoming *godlike*.

Jesus answered them, Is it not written in your law, I SAID, YE ARE GODS? If he called them gods, unto whom the word of God came... John 10:34

Now the parable is this: The seed is the word of God. Luke 8:11

It was through God's *word* that heaven and earth were made, as all things are made by a *seed*, the word of God being the works of creation. We were made in the image of God, coming into this world as gods, having the power to form a spiritual heaven and earth, which we have all done. This *"first heaven and earth"* was not made through God's word of truth, but through our own word of lies, bringing *"woe,* meaning *grief, misery,* the consequence of mistaking the darkness of a lie for the light of truth (Isaiah 5:20). It is through God's word, truth, that *"a new heaven and a new earth,"* symbolizing a new mind and a new heart, is made, the false perceptions and beliefs of our first heaven and earth, passing away. If we complete the works of this new creation by resurrecting truth in our mind and heart, we are of the first resurrection, coming forth in the city, in which no lie can ever exist (Revelation 21:27). If we have not completed the works by resurrecting truth in our mind and heart, we are of the second resurrection, in which we experience the second death; the death of our false perceptions and beliefs. Resurrection is of the dead. Which resurrection we take part in upon our physical death is determined by the degree of spiritual death that has taken place within us, corresponding to the degree of truth that has been resurrected within us, as Jesus, the truth personified, said, *"I am the resurrection."*

The teacher always encouraged us to go for the gold. He would often say, *"Put everything you have into it."* On those rare occasions when he taught on the reality of God's kingdom, he would talk about the benefits of being in the holy city. If your desire is to enjoy the company of a child, you enter the streets of Jerusalem, where the children play. If your desire is to travel the universe, you just go, as those in the city are not limited by any type of celestial flesh body.

But as it is written, Eye hath not seen, nor ear heard, neither have entered into the heart of man, the things which God hath prepared for them that love him. 1 Corinthians 2:9

So why not put everything we have into this life-changing process, demonstrating our love of God by removing our word of error, which formed the invisible sinful flesh that is limiting us in this life, and that will limit us in the afterlife. If we do the spiritual works we shall reap the greater rewards of both the physical and spiritual realms.

Chapter Thirteen
The Joseph Story

Joseph, a parallel to Jesus. He was hated by his biological brothers, as Jesus was hated by his religious brothers. He was falsely accused and thrown into prison, as was Jesus. But in the end, both would bring salvation to the people, Joseph giving them what they needed to preserve their physical life, and Jesus giving them what they needed to preserve their spiritual life. Joseph dwelt with his Hebrew brothers in the land of Canaan, as Jesus dwelt among his Jewish brothers in the land of Judea, both entering Egypt to save their own lives.

And when they were departed, behold, the angel of the Lord appeareth to Joseph in a dream, saying, Arise, take the young child and his mother, and flee into Egypt, and be thou there until I bring thee word: for Herod will seek the young child to destroy him. Matthew 2:13

Herod, the *king of Judah,* symbolizing the *spirit of the Heart,* is out to destroy the *Truth* of the heart, as Herod sought to destroy *Jesus,* and as Joseph's brothers sought to destroy him. Joseph's story centers around two groups of people: the Hebrews and the Egyptians. The Hebrews represent those adhering to the carnal-minded doctrines of religion. The Egyptians represent those that are spiritually-minded. The actions of Herod and the brothers of Joseph illustrate religion's attempt to destroy the spiritual Word of God. But God saw to its preservation, bringing it into Egypt, to the Egyptians; to those who are spiritually adept. God has kept

His spiritual Word alive over the ages through men and woman who served as pure conduits for this spiritual truth. There have always been human vessels through whom this ancient spiritual knowledge could be obtained. Joseph, like Jesus, was falsely accused and thrown into prison. It was in this solitude that Joseph came in contact with the baker and the butler, the *baker* symbolizing the *spirit* of God, and the *butler* symbolizing the *word* of God. Joseph became imbued with the *spirit of God*.

And Pharaoh said unto his servants, Can we find such a one as this is, a man in whom the Spirit of God is? Genesis 41:38

The spirit and word culminated in Joseph, as they would in Jesus. The *word* increases through the spirit, illustrated in the reinstating of the *butler*, while the *spirit*, having now become one with the word, decreases, as seen in the fate of the *baker* and John the Baptist. Both Joseph and Jesus had the double-portion of spirit and truth, having completed the spiritual works, through which the spirit and word of God reached their highest degree. At the age of thirty, the age required to become a high priest, Joseph sacrificed for the people, which is the duty of the high priest.

And Joseph was thirty years old when he stood before Pharaoh king of Egypt, and Joseph went out from the presence of Pharaoh and went throughout all the land of Egypt. Genesis 41:46

Jesus, at the age of thirty, went throughout all the land, sacrificing his time to teach the spiritual word of God, feeding the people with the spiritual corn, later sacrificed because of the iniquity of the people.

Behold, the days come, saith the Lord God, that I will send a famine in the land, not a famine of bread, nor a thirst for water, but of a hearing of the words of the Lord: Amos 8:11

Joseph made sacrifice for himself during his time in prison, putting him in a position to make sacrifice for the people, which he did by gathering in the corn that fed them during the *famine*.

And the seven years of dearth began to come, according as Joseph had said: and the dearth was in all lands: but in all the land of Egypt there was bread. Genesis 41:54

The Egyptians have *bread*, which means *to overcome*. The bread comes through Joseph, as the power to overcome the false perceptions and beliefs that are preventing us from receiving what we want out of life, comes by obeying the spiritual teachings of Jesus. The number *seven* is the *spiritual* number, indicating a spiritual dearth or famine. The Egyptians have bread. It's the Hebrews that are in a spiritual famine, where they will remain until they begin to eat of the knowledge of spiritual truth, fulfilling biblical scripture and prophecy from within. The literal interpretations of the carnal mind serve only to distract one from seeking the deeper spiritual truths contained in scripture, which reveal the spiritual events taking place in their mind and heart, as the Bible takes place within. People turn to religion to learn about God, but most religions take from the people the very thing they hoped to attain. With the famine waxing sore in all the lands, the Hebrews are forced to go down into Egypt to get the *corn*, symbolizing the *spiritual word of God*. To eat of the corn is to accept the word of God into ones heart by doing the spiritual works, which is already taking place among the Egyptians; in the minds and hearts of the un-indoctrinated people.

Now when Jacob saw that there was corn in Egypt, Jacob said unto his sons, Why do ye look one upon another? And he said, Behold I have heard that there is corn in Egypt: get you down thither, and buy for us from thence; that we may live, and not die. And Joseph's ten brothers went down to buy corn in Egypt. Genesis 42:1-3

Jacob symbolizes not only the *Spirit,* but the era of Spirit, the outpouring of which is creating a hunger for spiritual truth, motivating the ten brothers, those in bondage to the carnal-minded doctrines of religion, to humble themselves to *spiritual truth*, as the brothers, born of Leah and the bondmaids, symbolizing flesh and bondage, are about to humble themselves to *Joseph*. Jacob says to his sons, *"get you down,"* a humbleness that will get the religious brothers down to a symbolic Jordan. Once there, they will take part in a spiritual baptism, being immersed in *the name* of the Father, which is *truth, spiritual truth*. Through a circumcision of the ears and eyes, they will begin to eat of the old corn, which is to accept this ancient spiritual truth in their hearts, which has been stored up for the end times. They eat of the corn by doing the spiritual works of the Word, obtaining spiritual life. But before this takes place, they will have to feel the effects of the famine, which will take place when their spiritual appetites are no longer satisfied by the doctrines of religion. Or when they enter their time of trouble, which for many will not occur until they see that the carnal interpretations that were sold to them, do not match the reality of what is taking place in the world. This will force them into a spiritual famine, giving them a great desire to hear (obey) the spiritual word of the Lord, which is to eat of *"the old corn,"* the word *ear* meaning *to hear* (Joshua 5:12). The ten sons of Jacob that came against Joseph parallel the ten kings that give power to the beast and his image *"until the words of God shall be fulfilled"* (Revelation 17:17). The *words of God* are fulfilled through the spiritual works of God's Word, through which the beastly religious image is made desolate.

Behold, I will make them of the synagogue of Satan, which say they are Jews, and are not, but do lie; behold, I will make them to come and worship before thy feet, and to know that I have loved thee.

Revelation 3:9

A Jew is one born of Hebrew parents. The word *Hebrew* means *a region across, on the opposite side, esp. of the Jordan; to cross over, used widely of any transition.* We begin the process of becoming a spiritual Jew by crossing over a spiritual Jordan, as Abram crossed the Euphrates; our transition from carnal to spiritual mind, the twelve stones in the Jordan symbolizing the process that removes the flesh formed by our false images or beliefs, which is spiritual circumcision; the mark of a spiritual Jew. A Jew is one who believes; one who puts action to the spiritual Word of God through spiritual works, becoming a spiritual son (John 10:36-38). The *synagogue of Satan* is the *church,* where the spiritual works, through which one becomes a spiritual Jew, are not being taught. Jesus said, *"salvation is of the Jews"* (John 4:22), referring to the spiritual Jews. Abram and Sarai became Hebrews, in the positive sense, by crossing over from a land that worshipped images to the Promised Land, where they received the promise of Isaac, receiving the *son,* symbolizing the *seed* or *word* of God, receiving salvation.

And he said unto them, Hear, I pray you, this dream which I have dreamed: For, behold, we were binding sheaves in the field, and, lo, my sheaf arose, and also stood upright; and, behold, your sheaves made obeisance to my sheaf. And his brethren said to him, Shalt thou indeed reign over us? or shalt thou indeed have dominion over us? And they hated him yet the more for his dreams, and for his words.

Genesis 37:6-8

The brothers will bow down to Joseph, as those that *"say they are Jews";* say they believe, but do lie, will humble themselves to those that have kept the Word of God by doing the spiritual works. Those that think they have been keeping the Word or Law of God will come to know otherwise, and many of them will make *obeisance* to the Word or Law of God by acquiescing to its deeper spiritual truths. They will eat of the spiritual corn that will sustain their spiritual life, as the brothers lives were sustained by the corn they received at Joseph's hand.

And when the land of Egypt was famished, the people cried for bread: and Pharaoh said unto all the Egyptians, Go unto Joseph; what he saith to you, do. Genesis 41:55

And on the third day there was a marriage in Cana of Galilee; and the mother of Jesus was there:.. His mother saith unto the servants, Whatsoever he saith unto you, do it. John 2:1,5

Another parallel between Joseph and Jesus.

The time that Joseph was among his brothers in the land of Canaan, parallels the time that Jesus was among his Jewish brothers in the land of Judea. Joseph's brothers turned against him, as Jesus' religious brothers turned against him, Joseph and Jesus both hated for the words they spoke. Joseph was taken into Egypt after his brothers sought to murder him, as the child Jesus was taken into Egypt after Herod, king of Judah, sought to murder him. The *king* of Judah symbolizes the *spirit* that has gained power in Christianity through carnal-minded doctrines that served only to destroy the spiritual Word of God. Joseph being thrown in the pit illustrated the Jew's rejection of God's Word, which the Gentiles also rejected (Acts 4:27). The spiritual Word of God will continue to be rejected by those blinded by the carnal-minded doctrines of religion, as it is written, *"blindness in part is happened to Israel until the fullness of the Gentiles be come in."* A spiritual Gentile is one who has no preconceptions about the Word of God, or is willing to let go of the beliefs he does have. These spiritual Gentiles, open to this age-old spiritual truth, fall under the category of Egyptians, who are the first to eat of Joseph's corn. But as the spiritual famine increases, there will be many that will seek the word of the Lord, *and shall not find it.*

Behold, the days come, saith the Lord God, that I will send a famine in the land, not a famine of bread, nor a thirst for water, but of hearing the words of the Lord: And they shall wander from sea to sea, and from the north even to the east, they shall run to and fro to seek the word of the Lord, and shall not find it. Amos 8:11,12

They will not find it because they will be looking in the wrong place. The word of the Lord will not be found in religious Christianity. It's in Egypt, the last place Christians would ever think to look for it. *Egypt* symbolizes the *World,* and the *Egyptians,* the *worldly people,* a label placed on those deemed unworthy by so-called believers; those that say they believe, but do lie. The Egyptians are closer to hearing the spiritual word of God because they have no image with respect to God's Word. So while the Egyptians eat of Joseph's corn, accepting the word of God through spiritual works that bring spiritual life, the Hebrews are far removed from it due to their carnal-minded doctrines.

For if thou wert cut out of the olive tree which is wild by nature, and wert grafted in contrary to nature into a good olive tree: how much more shall these, which be the natural branches, be grafted into their own olive tree? Romans 11:24

The *natural branches* symbolize the *Jews and Christians,* those that have been introduced to the Law or Word of God through religion. If God is pleased to graft in the wild branches, those not of religion, how much more will it please Him to graft in those leaving doctrines that fail to teach the deeper spiritual truths of His Word? As the tribulation intensifies, so too will the spiritual famine, causing those deeply rooted in the error of religious doctrine, to hunger for spiritual truth. Many will come to know that they have been lied to. They will come to realize that there is no carnal deliverer coming to take them out of the time of trouble that is coming upon the world. They will come to hate the religious image, as the ten horns of the beast *"hate the whore... make her desolate... and burn her with fire"* (Revelation 17:16). The natural branches will have to humble themselves to accept this spiritual truth, as the ten brothers had to humble themselves to eat of Joseph's corn. But the corn the brothers receive from Joseph does not sustain them for long. To receive life that is more than temporal, life that is everlasting, they must bring down Benjamin.

Hereby shall ye be proved: By the life of Pharaoh, ye shall not go forth hence, except your youngest brother come hither. Send one of you, and let him fetch your brother, and ye shall be kept in prison, that your words may be proved, whether there be any truth in you: or else by the life of Pharaoh surely ye are spies. And he put them all together in ward three days. Genesis 42:15-17

The *three days* the brothers spent in ward is a parallel to the three days Jonah spent in the belly of the great fish, the consequence of disobeying the word of the Lord. The brothers of Joseph represent those that have disobeyed the word of the Lord by giving reverence to doctrines that failed to teach them about the spiritual works of salvation.

Bring your youngest brother unto me; so shall your words be verified, and ye shall not die. And they did so... And Reuben answered them, saying, Spake I not unto you, saying, Do not sin against the child; and ye would not hear? Therefore, behold, also his blood is required.
Genesis 42:20,22

Reuben symbolizes the part of us that wants to shift the blame or deny responsibility for our part in the dire situation we now find ourselves. But the days of justification and blame are over. The brothers were guilty of the intended death of Joseph, and now *his blood is required*. It's time to pay for the death of truth that has taken place in our heart.

And they knew not that Joseph understood them; for he spake unto them through an interpreter. Genesis 42:23

Joseph and Jesus understood their brothers' language, but the brothers, biological and religious, did not understand theirs. Joseph was speaking a different language, as was Jesus, speaking with a new, and yet, ancient, tongue, one that is foreign to the religious ear.

And he turned himself about from them, and wept; and returned to them again, and communed with them, and took from them Simeon, and bound him before their eyes. Genesis 42:24

Joseph was separated from his brothers for *20 years,* representing the past *2000 years,* in which religion and spiritual truth have remained separated. The rejection Joseph felt from his brothers was the type and shadow of what Jesus felt when his Father's spiritual teachings were rejected by his religious brothers. Like with Joseph, it was an emotionally painful experience, one compounded by the actions of the Gentiles, who also gathered themselves together against the spiritual word of God in the flesh. But now, after 2000 years, this spiritual truth is alive and well, living in *Egypt,* symbolizing the *World.* If the religious brothers humble themselves, admitting to their error, the word of God will commune with them, binding *Simeon,* the negative aspect of which is their word of error— their false religious beliefs.

And Joseph commanded to fill their sacks with corn, and to restore every man's money into his sack, and to give them provision for the way: and thus did he unto them. Genesis 42:25

They are given some corn, which is to give ear; to hear, to put action to the spiritual word or works of God. But their money is being returned to them. They will not satisfy their spiritual debt until they obey Joseph, and bring down Benjamin. The word *corn* has two meanings: *1. to clarify (i.e. brighten), examine, cleanse, (be clean), shew self pure, purge out. 2. a fracture, fig. ruin; specially a solution (of a dream):-affliction, crashing, destruction, vexation.* The corn in the brother's sacks takes its meaning from the latter, revealing what must take place in order to actualize the former. The mystery of Joseph's dream was solved when the brothers were forced by the famine to humble themselves before Joseph, who was in possession of the corn the brothers needed to sustain their life.

Joseph's Dream: Genesis 37: 9,10.

Two Distinct Groups of People

Yea, they have chosen their own ways, and their soul delighteth in their abominations. I also will choose their delusions, and will bring their fears upon them; because when I called, none did answer; when I spake, they did not hear: but they did evil before mine eyes, and chose that in which I delighted not...

Referencing one group of people— The Hebrews.

Hear the word of the Lord, ye that tremble at his word; Your brethren that hated you, that cast you out for my name's sake, said Let the Lord be glorified: but he shall appear to your joy, and they shall be ashamed.
Isaiah 66:3-5

Referencing the other group of people— The Egyptians.

And many of them that sleep in the dust of the earth shall awake, some to everlasting life, and some to shame and everlasting contempt.
Daniel 12:2

Again, we are being shown two very different experiences. This was also illustrated upon the birth of Jacob's last son, where Rachel calls him *Benoni,* meaning *son of my sorrow,* but Jacob calls him *Benjamin,* meaning *a son of the right hand,* the right hand symbolizing power.

Before she travailed, she brought forth; before her pain came, she was delivered of a man child... Shall the earth be made to bring forth in one day? or shall a nation be born at once?...

This describes one group of people— Judah. Those that say they are born again before going through the tribulation or pain of delivery. They omit the spiritual works or labor that brings them to the birth. They must bring down the negative aspect of Benjamin, which is the false image they have with regard to being born again, and begin the process that will bring forth the positive aspect of Benjamin.

...for as soon as Zion travailed, she brought forth her children.
Isaiah 66:6-8

The other group goes through the travailing that brings on the birth. Zion, unlike Judah, does it in the right order; *"after the order of Melchizedek;"* a spiritual order that must be followed to become a son of God, and a spiritual high priest, who having first made sacrifice for himself by carrying his own burden (Jeremiah 23:36), sacrificing his own lamb of unrighteousness, can now make sacrifice for the people, giving of his time to help others. A *son* symbolizes *full maturity,* standing in stark contrast to the untimely fruit of Judah. If we become a son through the completion of this spiritual process, we will be born again, born of the spirit, in the reality of God's kingdom, which takes place upon the death of that mother that is our physical flesh body, as *Benjamin,* meaning *a son of the right hand,* was born upon the death of his mother, a spiritual truth that was demonstrated for us when, upon the death of his flesh body, Jesus, the Son of God, sat on the right hand of God, being born of pure spirit (Luke 22:69; Heb. 8:1; 1 Pet.3:22).

Benjamin's Evil, Judgment, and Reformation

To understand the evil of Benjamin, their judgment, and what they must do to live, we must go to the book of Judges and read chapters nineteen through twenty one.

Overview: A man, a Levite, who has been dwelling on the side of mount Ephraim, takes a concubine to wife out of Bethleham-judah. His wife, who has committed whoredom, is separated from him for four months. After this time, he goes after her, spending time at the house of his father-in-law. On the fifth day, he departs from the house of his father-in-law, and goes to the house of the Lord. He comes near unto Jebus; ancient Jerusalem, but declines to spend even a night there, pressing on instead to Gibeah, where the ungodly men of Benjamin dwell. An old man, also of mount Ephraim, sees him, and invites him to lodge at his place.

Now as they were making their hearts merry, behold, the men of the city, certain sons of Belial, beset the house about, and beat at the door, and spake to the master of the house, the old man, saying, Bring forth the man that came into thine house that we may know him. Judges 19:22

The man is a Levite, the tribe of the carnal priesthood, indicating he is under the Law. He is of mount *Ephraim*, meaning *double fruit*, duality or two ways; carnal and spiritual. The Levite man remains in the house of his father-in-law until the fifth day, which is to remain under the carnal Law. Jesus came in the fifth day; in the beginning of the fifth thousandth year, *five* representing *taxation*, which is *to make a choice:* remain under the Law or come out from it, the choice they were taxed with two thousand years ago. The man chooses to come out from the Law, leaving the house of his father-in-law. He heads for Jerusalem, to the house of the Lord, but never enters, *Jerusalem* symbolizing the *Heart*. Instead, he ends up dwelling with the Benjaminites, the sons of *Belial*, meaning *without profit, worthlessness, destruction, wickedness, ungodly men*. These evil men want to have intercourse with him, illustrating their ungodly lust to sow the evil seeds of false beliefs. This same wickedness reverberates in the story of Sodom and Gomorrah.

And they called unto Lot, and said unto him, Where are the men which came in to thee this night? Bring them out unto us that we may know them. Genesis 19:5

The Biblical meaning of the word, *know*, is *sexual intercourse*. Spiritual intercourse is communication with the mind and heart. If we do not enter Jerusalem, the Heart, and purify it, through which the holy power of our heart is restored, we will be susceptible to the sowing of evil seeds; readily accepting false beliefs that make us feel empowered, but the belief is false, and its power, which is of the mind, unholy.

Behold, here is my daughter a maiden, and his concubine; them I will bring out now, and humble ye them, and do with them what seemeth good unto you: but unto this man do not so vile a thing. Judges 19:24

And Lot went out at the door unto them, and shut the door after him, And said, I pray you, brethren, do not so wickedly. Behold now, I have two daughters which have not known man; let me, I pray you, bring them out unto you, and do ye to them as is good in your eyes: only unto these men do nothing; for therefore came they under the shadow of my roof. Genesis 19:6-8

The *daughter*, a woman, symbolizes *flesh*, the *man* or *men* symbolizing the *inner being*. Defiling the inner being of God's spirit and word, is far more detrimental than defiling that which houses the inner being, the greater of the two evils.

But the men would not hearken to him: so the man took his concubine, and brought her forth unto them: and they knew her, and abused her all the night until the morning: and when the day began to spring, they let her go. Judges 19:25

Spiritual rape of the flesh takes place when untruthful seeds of thought are forced into the mind, repeatedly, which is taking place in far too many churches today. Lies are being forced into the minds of the people using fear, and that which is forced into the mind repeatedly, will, through the process of time and the power of emotion, becomes a seed, word, or belief of the heart, which is the seat of the *soul*.

For I have heard the voice as of a woman in travail, and the anguish as of her that bringeth forth her first child, the voice of the daughter of Zion, that bewaileth herself, that spreadeth her hands, saying, Woe is me now! For my soul is wearied because of murderers. Jeremiah 4:31

The *woman* symbolizes *flesh*. God's desire is for all humans, all flesh, to seek, and bring forth truth. Everyone that shares in this desire, or begins the spiritual works that makes it a reality, is a *daughter of Zion*. But many of these spiritual daughters are suffering *because of murderers;* because of religious leaders, whose carnal-minded doctrines have failed to teach the spiritual works of God's Word; an instruction, that if followed, would deliver them of that which is causing their soul to suffer.

Spiritual rape, which stifles the holy spirit, extinguishing the divine spark, is a horrific act committed against the soul. Seeds should always be sown through mutual desire. If someone attempts to *force* a belief upon us that we are not comfortable with, we would be wise to reject such a belief until we are drawn to it naturally, through the desire of our own heart, ensuring we never allow spiritual rape to be committed against our soul. Every evil seed or false belief sown into the heart is an evil act committed against the soul, causing injury, preventing the soul from achieving its highest potential, preventing the keeper of the soul from reaching perfection, reaching the highest degree, becoming the finest example of humankind, experiencing the highest degree of life in the both the physical and spiritual realm.

And Amnon said unto Tamar, Bring the meat into the chamber, that I may eat of thine hand. And Tamar took the cakes which she had made, and brought them into the chamber to Amnon her brother. And when she had brought them unto him to eat, he took hold of her, and said unto her, Come lie with me, my sister. And she answered him, Nay, my brother, do not force me; for no such thing ought to be done in Israel: do not this folly. 2 Samuel 13:10-12

The word *force* means *in the sense of browbeating, to depress*. The word browbeat means to intimidate or subject with an overbearing or imperative manner; domineer. The word imperative means to have the power or authority to command or control. Many join a church, a physical representation of the house of God, to be taught God's Word, which would take them on a journey through their own mind and heart. But what takes place far too often in these churches is spiritual rape, committed by those that have been given power and authority to greatly influence the minds of the flock. A doctrine is forced upon the followers in a domineering manner, oftentimes the members of the congregation made to feel inferior or stupid if they do not readily accept the beliefs that are being sold to them. Fear is the tool used to force the people into accepting the false doctrine. This forcing of ideas using fear comes down to a desperate need for control on the part of the leader, revealing his own lack of authentic power or holy spirit.

And from the days of John the Baptist unto now the kingdom of heaven suffereth violence, and the violent take it by force... Matthew 11:12

The *kingdom of heaven* symbolizes the *realm of the mind,* where we are first introduced to God. Sadly, it is suffering *violence* through the forcing of false doctrines. The men of Benjamin raped the woman until *the day began to spring,* revealing that this spiritual rape will continue until the one being raped comes into the light of it, understanding what is actually taking place. Truth is the reason many join the church, and the soul desires truth in order to be healed. But too many have come to associate truth or God's word with the church, where unfortunately there is still a great spiritual slaughter taking place.

A wonderful and horrible thing is committed in the land; The prophets prophesy falsely, and the priests bear rule by their means; and my people love to have it so: and what will ye do in the end thereof?
Jeremiah 5:30,31

It is a horrible thing that is being committed in the land of religion. Yet it will be wonderful if the people see it, and come out of it with their spirit and soul intact. This forcing of beliefs or spiritual rape wearies the soul by wearing us down mentally and emotionally. But it can only destroy the soul by preventing its healing if we allow it to get that far. This is why we must gather all of our strength together and destroy these childish beliefs, which are out to defile and destroy our soul. Through our desire for spiritual truth, the light of understanding will come, and hopefully in plenty of time to afford us the opportunity, in this lifetime, to bring our soul into its highest state of existence.

So all the men of Israel were gathered together against the city, knit together as one man. And the tribes of Israel sent men through all the tribe of Benjamin, saying, What wickedness is this that is done among you? Now therefore deliver us the men, the children of Belial, which are in Gibeah, that we may put them to death, and put away evil from

Israel. But the children of Benjamin would not hearken to the voice of their brethren the children of Israel. Judges 20:11-13

Israel symbolizes the *Mind,* which is now being strengthened to fight against the enemy that is the false belief. But it won't be easy for those who have been indoctrinated with these beliefs. As with the brothers of Joseph, it will take a prolonged famine, which will force them to bring down Benjamin; to bring down the false religious image or belief that they have accepted into their heart as truth, but which in fact, is a lie.

And the children of Israel went up and wept before the Lord until even, and asked counsel of the Lord, saying, Shall I go up again to battle against the children of Benjamin my brother? And the Lord said, Go up against him. Judges 20:23

The *children of Israel* symbolize the *unskilled of Mind.* Being unskilled in the Word of God, they are now asking counsel of the Lord, which is answering them, saying, YES, go up and battle against the children of Benjamin; against the evil (negative and destructive) childish "born again" belief, evidence of the unskilled mind.

And the Lord smote Benjamin before Israel: and the children of Israel destroyed of the Benjaminites that day twenty and five thousand and an hundred men: all these drew the sword. Judges 20:35

When the negative meaning of Benjamin; believing one is born again before completing the process of spiritual birth, is destroyed, the positive meaning of Benjamin; the birth of spirit through the completion of the spiritual judgment represented in the twelve tribes of Israel, can become a reality.

And the children of Israel repented them for Benjamin their brother, and said, There is one tribe cut off from Israel this day. How shall we do for wives for them that remain, seeing we have sworn by the Lord that we will not give them of our daughters to wives... And they found among the inhabitants of Jabesh-Gilead four hundred young virgins, that had known no man by lying with any male: and they brought them unto the camp to Shiloh, which is in the land of Canaan. Judges 21:6,7,12

The wives of Benjamin will be of Jabesh-Gilead. The word *Jabesh* means *to be ashamed or confused.* The word *Gilead* means *heap of testimony; heap of stones.* Benjamin, in the negative, is the false religious born again belief. The word *Benjamin* means *son of the right hand,* the right hand symbolizing power, which is what Christians are claiming to be when they say they are *born of the spirit* or *born again.* When they become ashamed of this childish belief, or it becomes a point of confusion for them, they will begin taking the twelve metaphorical steps through the twelve tribes of Israel, symbolized by the twelve stones placed in the Jordan, heaped up as a testimony to the spiritual judgment (Matthew 19:28) that consumes our false beliefs; consuming the flesh that fights against the spirit. We will have reached Benjamin in the positive, being born of the spirit in the reality of God's kingdom. When the heart is made pure though the elimination of every false belief it enters a *virgin* state, conceiving of God's word of truth, a spiritual seed, that when separated from the flesh body, will bring forth Benjamin, a son of the right hand; a son of the power of God. Those of us that work to reach this perfected state experience *Shiloh,* meaning *to be tranquil, secure, successful, be happy, prosper, be in safety;* describing our physical existence.

Two Distinct Inheritances

And the lot of the tribe of the children of Benjamin came up according to their families: and the coast of their lot came forth between the children of Judah and the children of Joseph. Joshua 18:11

For Judah prevailed above his brethren, and of him came the chief ruler; but the birthright was Joseph's. 1 Chronicles 5:2

Benjamin takes its inheritance between *Judah* (iniquity) and *Joseph* (truth). Judah is the tribe from which Jesus, the spiritual *chief ruler,* sprang. But Judah also represents the religious faction that started this born again lie to begin with; iniquity that has *prevailed,* permeating all of mainstream Christianity, causing many to forfeit their spiritual birthright. The *birthright* belongs to *Joseph;* to those that overcome the negative aspects of the sons of Leah and the bondmaids, symbolizing flesh and bondage. They become pure spirit through the removal of all flesh, being born of the spirit upon their physical death.

Therefore they commanded the children of Benjamin, saying, Go and lie in wait in the vineyards; And see, and, behold, if the daughters of Shiloh come out to dance in dances, then come ye out of the vineyards, and catch you every man his wife of the daughters of Shiloh, and go to the land of Benjamin... And the children of Benjamin did so, and took them wives... and they went and returned to their inheritance, and repaired the cities, and dwelt in them. Judges 21:20,22,23

The *vineyard* brings forth the fruit needed to make *wine,* symbolizing *spirit.* The holy *spirit,* the positive aspect of Benjamin, has been cut off, and must be replenished. At the marriage in Cana, only the *water* that was drawn out was turned to *wine.* Only those that are drawn up out of the *waste,* out of the iniquity, will be turned to *spirit.* Wine, like spirit, requires a process. Before we can be born of the spirit our holy spirit must be revitalized, quickened, giving it new life and vigor through God's purification or healing process.

Many pastors have destroyed my vineyard, they have trodden my portion under foot, they have made my pleasant portion a desolate wilderness.
Jeremiah 12:10

For the pastors have become brutish, and have not sought the Lord: therefore they shall not prosper, and all their flocks shall be scattered.
Jeremiah 10:21

God is not against the church, or the congregation. He is against the iniquity that is being fed to His people. These lies are keeping His people from the knowledge of His spiritual truth, as it is written, *"My people are destroyed for lack of knowledge"* (Hosea 4:6); spiritual knowledge, which through its application, restores spiritual life. If the *pastors* of these churches would completely clear their minds of the doctrine that was sold to them, they would give power to the holy spirit of the heart, which would bring them into the light of God's spiritual truth. They would then be able to lead their flock into the kingdom of heaven, and into the kingdom of God. If the heart of the religious leader is in the right place, which is to truly help the people, they will do the right thing. But if they are in it to feed their own ego, for control, or money, they will not. Each leader will have to make a choice. Become as David, loving and tending their flock by giving them the spiritual drink and the spiritual meat, or remain as Saul, demanding their flock sacrifice their time and money, giving them nothing in return but lies and false peace.

Woe be to the pastors that destroy and scatter the sheep of my pasture! saith the Lord. Therefore thus saith the Lord God of Israel against the pastors that feed my people. Ye have scattered my flock, and driven them away, and have not visited them: behold, I will visit upon you the evil of your doings saith the Lord. And I will gather the remnant of my flock out of all the countries whither I have driven them, and will bring them again to their folds; and they shall be fruitful and increase. And I will set up shepherds over them which shall feed them: and they shall fear no more, nor be dismayed, neither shall they be lacking saith the Lord.

Jeremiah 23:1-4

The Joseph story ends with the brothers doing what Joseph has instructed them to do, which is to bring down Benjamin. This gives me great hope. It tells me that in time, as the spiritual famine continues to intensify; those that remain under the energy of delusion will see through these false religious beliefs, and give them up. They will go down and dwell among the Egyptians, eating of the same corn by accepting the spiritual word of God into their heart through spiritual works. This will bring reconciliation between their own mind and heart, bringing *unity* within, which if actualized in enough of us, will bring *unity* without. We will no longer see nation lifting up sword against nation (Isaiah 2:4; Micah 4:3). We will beat our swords into plowshares as each of us concentrates on preparing our spiritual earth for the sowing of God's spiritual seed or word of truth. When there is truth in the heart of man, there will be peace in the earth. There will be no more wars within, or without (James 4:1). It will be like it was after the flood; after the receding of man's iniquity, and before the building of Babel; before the confusion of man's mind. When all men spoke the same language, the spiritual language of truth!

Behold, how good and how pleasant it is for brethren to dwell together in unity! It is like the precious ointment upon the head, that ran down upon the beard, even Aaron's beard: that went down to the skirts of his garments: As the dew of Hermon, and as the dew that descendeth upon the mountains of Zion: for there the Lord commanded the blessing, even life for evermore. Psalms 133:1-3

By forming ourselves into a new creation, becoming the true image in which we were made, we ascend into the kingdom of God; into the reality of Joseph. The word *Joseph* means *let him add*, and what has been added to our heart is truth. *Joseph* and *Benjamin* are the sons of Rachel, the one Jacob loved, as the Spirit loves the *Heart*, which *Rachel* symbolizes, the good fruit of the heart being *Truth* and *Spirit,* the two divine attributes of God; the image of God. Spirit is the power that brings us truth, and truth, which purifies the heart, perfects the spirit. Truth is life, providing us with an abundant life here on earth. We experience this new abundant life after we are separated from our spiritual mother of spiritual flesh, just as we experienced our new physical life after we were separated from our physical mother of physical flesh. The life of the body begins at conception. The life of the soul begins when we take our first breath. Before we take in the breath of life, we are just flesh, borrowing life from our mother. The soul is the life, not the flesh body!

And God formed man of the dust of the ground, and breathed into his nostrils the breath of life; and man became a living soul. Genesis 2:7

At resurrection, the spiritual kingdom that exists within us; be it darkness, a degree of light, or pure light, will translate to the reality of God's kingdom. If we have reached that ascended state called *christ;* spirit and truth in its highest degree, we will receive eternal life, as the word *Jehovah* means *self-Existent or Eternal.* We will enter the reality of Benjamin, which is to be born of the spirit, born from above.

YHWH said: My rushing-spirit shall not remain in human-kind for ages, for they too are flesh; let their days be then an hundred and twenty years! The giants were on earth in those days, and afterward as well, when the divine beings came in to the human women and they bore them [children]-they were the heroes who were of former ages, the men of name.
Genesis 6:3,4 (The Five Books of Moses)

Humankind took on the limitations of physical and spiritual flesh through physical and spiritual disobedience. The *giants* are those that have reached the highest degree of spiritual growth, a spiritual stature, becoming the finest example of humankind. The *human women* symbolize *human hearts* (female), which did not resist the divine *beings*; holy spirit that sows holy seed (male), through which the heart conceives, bearing *men of name; men of truth*. We might be amazed at what is possible once we obey the spiritual teachings of God's Word, escaping the spirit of disobedience that has possessed us for the past six thousand years.

Epilogue

The new millennium brought in the new era, the era of Jacob or era of Spirit. *"In the last days... I will pour out [of] my Spirit upon all flesh."* What is important is what we do with the power of spirit. Some externalize spirit through a technique called channeling, invoking spirits from the past, while others use spirit, which is activated by emotion, to dabble in past life regression. If we use spirit to get in touch with what we need to heal from the past of this life, it's holy, and we do well. Mediums have the ability to put us in touch with our spirit guides, whose highest purpose is to guide us into an understanding of our own spirit, so that we may align it with God's spirit. Through spirit, they bring through messages that can help us move forward in life, releasing us from any self-destructive thoughts or feelings that may have resulted from some traumatic experience. But if we are using the spiritual realm for our own entertainment, for any other purpose than the healing of the soul, it's unholy, and we are doing our self or others a great disservice, and great spiritual harm. There are two powers, two energies or spirits: the energy of delusion empowered by the mind's ego, and the spirit of truth, empowered by the heart's humility. The former seeks external power, power at the mind level, providing an illusion of peace, an attempt to fill the void created in the heart due to a loss of authentic power. The latter seeks internal power, power at the heart level, providing authentic peace and power through the revitalizing of the holy spirit of the heart. Those in whom the spirit is being poured out will experience those things associated with the internal outpouring of the spirit: prophesy, visions, dreams, wonders in heaven, and signs in the earth. (Joel 2:28). Their visions will be for the purpose of seeing themselves, seeing the workings of their own mind. Their dreams will become the means by which they come to understand their own emotional state, becoming self-empathic, aware of their own feelings, thoughts, and motives. The wonders they see in *heaven* will be the marvelous works they see taking place in their own *mind,* while the signs of the *earth* point to the marvelous changes taking place in their own *heart*.

"For it is written that Abraham had two sons." the son of the Hagar, the bondwoman, and the son of Sarah, the freewoman. In externalizing the power of the spirit we remain in bondage, because it is only by internalizing the power of the spirit that we come into the light of what is keeping us from being completely free in mind, heart, and body. Abraham goes on to have six more sons with Keturah, having to do with the gifts of the spirit; abilities evoked through the spirit, but by way of the mind. Hagar, Sarah, and Keturah represent three phases. *Hagar* is associated with the *mind and body;* with disciplines of the mind, such as prayers, incantations, affirmations, meditations and the like, which bring peace to the mind, and with disciplines of the body, such as the practice of yoga, which brings well-being to the body. *Sarah* is associated with the *heart;* with a heart discipline that transforms or purifies the heart, bringing authentic peace. *Keturah* is also associated with the *mind and body,* with

spiritual gifts, those abilities that require the disciplining of the mind and body to be achieved. We might be at peace in our mind, able to read the thoughts and feelings of others, or leave our body to travel the astral plane. But if we seek the gifts of the first and third phase at the exclusion of the gift of the second phase, we ultimately limit ourselves, because these abilities cannot bring us into a pure spiritual state of being.

*And Abraham gave all that he had unto Isaac. **But unto the sons of the concubines, which Abraham had, Abraham gave gifts, and sent them away from Isaac his son… Genesis 25:5,6***

Abraham gave gifts to the sons of Hagar and Keturah. But unto Isaac, the son of Sarah, he gave all of his inheritance. All that the Father has will be given to those that complete the spiritual works. Those that do the works of purifying their heart will take part in an internal ascension, entering into the pure light of the fifth dimension from within their own heart. If we have skipped over the important heart work because of some false religious belief, or because we have put all of our time and energy into pursuing other gifts of the spirit, but now desire to receive the greatest gift of the spirit, we must enter the kingdom of God within, where we complete the spiritual works of God's Word. The works of the spirit may have the power to heal the mind and body. But it takes the works of the God's Word to heal the heart, which is the salvation of the soul.

A supplement to THE BIBLE DECODED

THE LITTLE BOOK for the soul
an ancient healing process

The detailed account of the ancient healing process encoded in the Holy Bible. God, knowing the condition in which we would find ourselves in the end of days has left us with a transformation process that combines the ancient practices of the east with the ancient instruction found in the Sacred Text of the west. Through the creation story in the beginning of Genesis and Jacob's last words to his 12 sons in the end of Genesis we are given the blueprints for building a new life, the negative and destructive energy responsible for our many disorders, addictions, and diseases transformed into positive and constructive energy. It is a process that brings salvation through christ, providing the best and highest degree of life in the physical and spiritual realm. The power to perform this healing has been with us all along. It is simply a matter of activating it according to God's ancient instruction, presented in the pages of this little book for the healing of the soul.

There are different names given to this process by those adhering to different beliefs. Some call it salvation or purification; others refer to it as ascension or spiritual birth. Whatever you choose to call it, there is none as complete as the one brilliantly encoded in *The Holy Bible*.

Book References

The Authorized King James Version of the Bible

The Five Books of Moses - The Schocken Bible Volume 1

The Emphatic Diaglott

The New Strong's Exhaustive Concordance of the Bible *by James Strong, LL.D, S.T.D.*

Heal Your Body *by Louise L. Hay*

The American Heritage Dictionary

Funk & Wagnalls New Encyclopedia

Index to Scripture References

Genesis
1:1......1
1:2.......1, 6
1:3, 4. 1
1:6-9 2
1:10 ......2, 23
1:11 3
1:12, 13 4
1:24 8
1:26 5
1: 27 6,135
2:7 ......9, 220
2:17, 18 10
3:2-5 12
3:9-11 139
3:17, 18.....4
3:21 ......14, 139
6:3 ......138, 220
6:4 220
9:25 46
11:1-6 115
11:7-9 116
15:1-10 120
15:17 121
15:18-21 122
17:12 162
19:5-8 211
25:5, 6 222
25:22 128
25:30 ......11, 26, 112, 148
25:31-34 ......26, 148
31:41......165
36:8 ......102, 112
37:6-8 203
37:9, 10 ......149, 183, 208
38:1, 2 79
38:7-9 80
38:28-30 83
40:16-22 ......98 , 99

41:38, 46 200
41:54 201
41:55 204
42:1-3 201
42:15-17 206
42:20, 22-25 206,207
47:15 54
49:1 151
49:3 136
49:8-10 91

Exodus
2:10 ......20, 71
2:23 22
3:5 36
4:10 98
4:22 136
12:3 157
12:5-11 158-161
12:16-18 164,165
12:21, 27.....167
12:27 174
14:10, 11 ......24, 69
14:12 69
14:13.....23
14:16 23
14:31 24
15:26 147
15:27 25
16:19 160
17:4 26
19:1-11 ......26, 27
19:10-15 36
19:16 27
20:3-5 ......44, 57, 61
20:7......96
20:13......158
20:14 51

Index to Scripture References

20:15 157
20:20-24 28
33:23 138
34:34, 35 32

Deuteronomy
23:2 76
34:7 138

Joshua
3:10 38
3:15, 16 33
5:1, 2 34
5:12 202
5:9-12 ......34, 35
5:10 164
5:15 36
6:1 37
6:3-5 37
6:26 41
7:1 ......42, 164
7 21 42
15:63 81
18:11 216
23:11-16 44
24:15 81

Judges
18:31 156
19:22 210
19:24, 25 211
20:11-13 214
20:23 215
20:35 215
21:6, 7, 12 215
21:20, 22, 23 217

1 Samuel
2:12, 17….. 97

2:34, 35 97
4:11 97
4:15-18 101
4:19-22 98
8:6-20 ......61, 62
8:7 51
13:14 162
15:26, 28 66
29:5 67

2 Samuel
3:10 51
5:4, 5 67
6:3, 12 102
13:10-12 213
21:1 83

1 Kings
11:1-4 67
12:10, 11 85
19:5 98
19:7, 8 99
22:4 88

2 Kings
2:9 200
6:6 124
11:1-21 192
13:21 32
20:5, 6 95
23:22 163
25:24 127

1 Chronicles
5:2 216

2 Chronicles
34:1-5 162

Index to Scripture References

Job
38:4-8 11

Psalms
27:5 153
31:7, 8 110
51:5 ......14, 145, 187
51:6 ......145, 187
51:10-12 ......40, 143, 189
51:13 189
51:17......28, 97, 143, 189
51:18 143
110:4 209
122:3, 5-8.....144
132:13, 14 113
133:1-3 219

Proverbs
23:7 174
26:25 ......38, 104, 178

Isaiah
1:4 103
1:8 109
1:9 103
2:3 113
2:4 219
3:16, 17, 26 105
4:1 ......35, 107
4:2, 3 111
5:1-6. 84
5:7 86
5:20 ......2, 7, 169, 196
6:9, 10 32
7:14 ......40, 73, 166
30:20-22 106
37:3 148
38:1-5 125
45:7 2
46:13 103
53:5 ......132, 158
55:8, 9 13
66:3-5 208
66:6-8 209
66:7, 8 ......88, 147, 173

Jeremiah
2:19 ......90, 131
2:28 86
3:8 51
3:6-8 82
3:6-14 ......55, 56
3:11-15 96
4:4 ......15, 181
4:18, 19 130
4:31 212
5:24 177
5:30 214
5:31 ......65, 214
8:20 173
10:21 217
11:12 152
12:10 217
23:1-4 218
23:34 132
23:36.....21, 132, 142, 209
25:1, 8, 9 125
27:14 127
30:5-8 151
51:6 133
51:60-64 128

Index to Scripture References

Ezekiel
4:4-6 ......29, 80, 81
13:10-16 ......140, 141
21:21 130

Daniel
2:31-35 ......116, 124
2:37, 38, 39 117
2:40-43 118
2:44 119
7:7 118
9:2 139
9:24 ......25, 78, 126
12:1 ......145, 148
12:2 214
12:10 191

Hosea
4:6 218
9:14 105

Joel
2:1 149
2:23, 24......172
2:28 221
3:15 183

Amos
8:11 ......19, 200, 205
8:12 211

Obadiah
1:21.......113

Jonah
1:1-3 155
1:17 156

Micah
4:3 219

Zechariah
13:6 110

Malachi
3:8 157

Matthew
1:3-12 83
2:13 199
3:1, 2 175
3:13-15 71
4:1, 2 175
4:15-17 170
5:3 189
5:20 171
6:24 53
6:33 174
9:14 175
9:37 173
11:12 213
12:28 179
12:40 25
12:43-45 ......39, 178, 179
13:24-30 172
13:33 171
13:47, 48 169
15:19.....38, 104, 178
15:20 178
16:19 174
18:1-4 173
19:28 ......120, 140, 143, 182, 188, 216
22:12, 13 191
23:9 86

Index to Scripture References

23:25 171
23:26 ......49, 171
24:1, 2 139
24:23, 24 191
24:29 149
24:30 131
26:18, 21 163
27:29......75
27:45 155
27:50, 51 142
28:19 70

Mark
1:15 179
4:11 129
4:30-32 181
5:8, 9 179
6:21-27 99
13:24-27 149
16:9 ......39, 179

Luke
3:16, 17 72
5:33 176
6:41, 42 46
6:45 76
7:28 177
8:11 ......4, 196
17:20, 21......66, 174
21:19 89
22:69 209

John
1:14 160
1:32 176
2:1, 5 204
2:6-9 16
2:13-15 ......52, 164

2:16 ......52, 156, 164
2:19, 20......68, 135
3:5-8 180
3:30 ......99, 176
4:1, 2 70
4:21-23 ...... 65, 203
4:24......65, 151
5:43 ......70, 76
8:44 157
10:32-38 ......5, 60, 176, 178, 203
11:25 197
14:12 176
15:17-25 108
16:1-3 109
16:13 ......65, 181

Acts
1:9-11 ......131, 132
1:18-20 ......42, 164
2:1-4 72
2:17 ......17, 221
2:18, 19 221
2:38 ......70, 83
4:26, 27 ......57, 204
7:51 190
10:48 70
19:26-28 58

Romans
1:20 5
1:21-25 13
6:23 164
8:6......12
9:7 76
11:8 ......166, 172
11:24, 25...... 204, 205
11:26, 27 111
14:17 181

230

Index to Scripture References

1 Corinthians
2:9 197
3:1-3 63
10:1 ......31, 59
10:2 31
10:3, 4 ......59, 102
11:31 188
15:35-40 190
15:45 ......8, 9, 17, 89, 153

2 Corinthians
3:3 ...... 53, 164

Galatians
4:4 135
4:15 136
4:19 173
4:21 ......31, 167
4:22 ......22, 137, 222
4:23 ......137, 181
4:24 22
4:25 136
4:26 76
4:30 187
4: 31 36
5:17 138
5:18...... 138
5:19-21 179

2 Thessalonians
2:11 ......112, 218

1 Timothy
4:1-3 86
6:10 53

Hebrews
6:1, 2 176
7:11 ......34, 161
7:12-14 34
8:1 209
9:27 188
11:1 177
12:26 148

James
1:22-24 40
2:15-17 177
4:1 ......175, 219
4:8 175

1 Peter
1:9, 10 178
3:22 209

2 Peter
2:20 96
2:21, 22 50
3:8 ......17, 101, 102

1 John
2:27 64
4:18 73

Revelation
2:4 51
2:10 150
2:17 107
2:26, 27.....123
3:1 37
3:2 ......37, 143, 166
      178, 187

Index to Scripture References

3:9 202
3:10 150
3:12 ......144, 163, 182
3:18 12 139
6:12 142
6:13 148
7:1-3 150
7:4 182
7:13-15 151
10:7-11 129
11:3, 7, 8 ......152, 153
11:9 20
11:11 ......22, 100
13:1 126
13:5 54
13:11, 12 89
13:17, 18 54
15:1, 2 ......127, 128
15:8 140
16:9-11 152
16:12 128
16:13, 14 191
16:19 121
17:3...... 60
17:5 ......117, 129

17:7......58, 202
17:9, 10 60
17:12, 13.....123
17:16 206
17:17 202
18:2 122
18:11 58
20:4, 5 188
20:6 189
20:7 191
20:8-10 192
20:11, 12 193
20:13-15 195
21:1 ......17, 41, 73, 144, 164, 182, 196
21:4 144
21:5 73
21:8 196
21:9 182
21:17 ......144, 182
21:23-26 183
21:27 ......147, 183, 197
22:1, 2, 17......184

www.ingramcontent.com/pod-product-compliance
Lightning Source LLC
Chambersburg PA
CBHW020925090426
42736CB00010B/1044